"Jesus led through weakness and whispered to Paul, 'My power is made perfect through weakness.' Yet, as his under-shepherds, we all too often sacrifice all on the altar of strength, performance, and success. Peter Ahn, a brother I both love and respect, invites us to courageously embrace a pathway of surrendered vulnerability that not only invites our Christ to pour his power through us—but also invites wounded sons and daughters of God . . . to come home. I only wish I had *The Weak Church* 40 years ago!!"

—**J. Kevin Butcher**, Founder CEO of Rooted Pastors, and author of *Free: Rescued from Shame Based Religion, Released into the Life-Giving Love of Jesus*

"True strength is found in weakness. Peter Ahn makes a powerful case for how it is in our weakness that we are made strong—and made strong because we create space for the Holy Spirit to move and create space for bonds of fellowship to form. Ahn models and maps out the power of a weak church, a church that makes room for God's strength to surface and shine. Ahn draws from his own experiences and the experiences of Metro Community Church to show that these aren't mere platitudes, but truly possible—and in so doing, allows God to be glorified in our vulnerability, humility, and authenticity. If you've ever wondered what Paul meant when he said, 'When I am weak, I am strong,' *The Weak Church* paints a profound picture and provides practical steps towards it."

—**Rev. Raymond Chang**, president, Asian American Christian Collaborative

"As the strength of a chain is measured by its weakest link, the strength of a person or community is also measured by how it engages its weakness. *The Weak Church* critiques the hubris of modern church life, challenging its basis in performative boasting, rather than in demonstrating the power of God that transforms weakness into humble strength."

—**Howard K. Burgoyne**, East Coast Superintendent, Evangelical Covenant Church

The WEAK Church

The WEAK Church

Becoming an Imperfectly Perfect Community

Peter Ahn

Foreword by Eugene Cho

t&tclark

NEW YORK · LONDON · OXFORD · NEW DELHI · SYDNEY

T&T CLARK

Bloomsbury Publishing Inc, 1385 Broadway, New York, NY 10018, USA
Bloomsbury Publishing Plc, 50 Bedford Square, London, WC1B 3DP, UK
Bloomsbury Publishing Ireland, 29 Earlsfort Terrace, Dublin 2, D02 AY28, Ireland

BLOOMSBURY, T&T CLARK and the T&T Clark logo are trademarks of Bloomsbury
Publishing Plc

First published in the United States of America 2025

Cover design: Diana Nuhn
Cover image © iStock/tombilla

Library of Congress Cataloging-in-Publication Data

ISBN: HB: 978-1-5381-9967-1
       PB: 978-1-5381-9968-8
     ePDF: 979-8-7651-5528-8
    eBook: 978-1-5381-9969-5

Typeset by Deanta Global Publishing Services, Chennai, India
Printed and bound in the United States of America

For product safety related questions contact productsafety@bloomsbury.com.

To find out more about our authors and books visit www.bloomsbury.com and sign up for
our newsletters.

With deep love, gratitude, and respect, I dedicate this book to my mother, In Soon Ahn, and my late father, Chul Kyu Ahn. As an immigrant family courageously navigating the challenges of building a new life in America, you loved me to the best of your ability and instilled in me the values of grit, tenacity, culture, and perseverance. Your sacrifices and resilience profoundly shaped who I am, and it is because of you that I've come to understand the supernatural power of embracing my weakness with humility, leading to eternal hope.

책의 헌사

깊은 사랑과 감사, 그리고 존경의 마음을 담아 이 책을 저의 어머니
안인순 여사와 고인이 되신 아버지 안철규님께 바칩니다.
이민자 가정으로서 미국에서 새로운 삶을 개척하는 여정 속에서,
부모님은 최선을 다해 저를 사랑해 주셨고, 끈기와 강인함,
그리고 문화와 인내의 가치를 몸소 가르쳐 주셨습니다.
특히 두 분의 희생과, 역경속에서도 소망을 잃지 않고 다시
일어서시는 모습은 제 인격 형성에 지대한 영향을 끼쳤습니다.
두 분을 통해 저는 저의 연약함을 겸손히 받아들일 수 있는 초월적인
능력이 영원한 소망으로 이어진다는 것을 이해하게 되었습니다. 이러한
깊은 삶의 지혜를 알게 해 주신 부모님께 진심으로 감사드립니다.

Contents

Foreword

I know what you're thinking: Do we need another book on leadership or church methodology?

Let's be honest. There's an overabundance of books on and about leadership today. In fact, there are over 70,000 books on Amazon with "leadership" *just* in the title. But it doesn't end there. In addition to books, there are gatherings, seminars, sermon series, and entire conferences around the subject of leadership—including within the church and ministry world.

And I get it. As a local church pastor for nearly thirty years and a leader in various organizations, I fully understand and acknowledge that leadership matters.

But I want you to know that *The Weak Church* by Peter Ahn is unlike any other book I've ever read on the topic of leadership or church ministry.

In fact, I don't think I've read anything similar to this book and thus I feel it's important for me to be honest here and say that readers should be warned.

I didn't necessarily "enjoy" the book.

I know that it's strange to state that about a book that you've been invited to write a foreword for, but let me clarify:

Conviction . . . isn't typically an enjoyable experience.

And I was deeply convicted by this book.

Seriously, when was the last moment you came across church models or ministry leadership that was rooted in the biblical basis of weakness? Not a page, or even a chapter, but the entire book focused on weakness as a path to reliance on Jesus?

Typically, we equate "robust church" and leadership with words and concepts like strong, visionary, growth, charismatic, accomplished, influential/influencer, successful, catalytic, dynamic, and the list goes on. These are the reasons why pastors and leaders wrestle with both the internal and external pressure and expectations of strength: bigger budgets, bigger crowds, bigger audiences, bigger followings, bigger platforms, bigger programs, bigger buildings, and ultimately all equating to the perception of bigger success.

Ahn isn't suggesting that these aforementioned metrics in themselves aren't bad, per se, but if we are not wise and careful, these very things become our north star—rather than our identities as children of God and reliance on Jesus. When metrics become our north star, they become our identities and "fruit" become metrics by which we compare ourselves to others.

Additionally, Ahn's sheer vulnerability and transparency about weakness left me speechless and at times uneasy and uncomfortable. He shares things in this book that I've rarely, if ever, read or heard publicly shared by another pastor.

Ahn confesses to the temptation of inflating numbers, embellishing stories, and obsessing with growth. He shares about wrestling with self-harm ideation, struggling with shame, spiritual lust for fame and prestige, and even writes about thinking of committing adultery during a dark season of his leadership.

Yes, he shares all of this—and more—in this book.

I wonder how many of us in ministry and leadership might read this book—and in the process, see a mirror.

Clearly, this is a challenging time in the Church for many complex reasons. There are seismic shifts and changes. There are scandals that have rocked the Church. There's intense division and polarization. There's significant decline in church attendance and relevance. And I fear that many will again resort to "best" or "effective" or "robust" practices in an attempt to revitalize the Church—and if so, we might be missing the message of the Gospel:

> Each time he said, "My grace is all you need. My power works best in weakness." So now I am glad to boast about my weaknesses, so that the power of Christ can work through me. (2 Corinthians 12:9 NLT)

No, I didn't necessarily enjoy the book but . . . I can say that *I needed this book*. And I believe the message of *The Weak Church* is an essential message for the Church and its leaders.

What we need today isn't more formulaic how-tos from self-professing gurus. We don't need more dazzling storytellers, we need more genuine storytellers. We need leaders who embrace their weakness, who confess and profess, and who desperately rely on the grace and power of God.

May it be so . . . and may it begin with me.

Rev. Eugene Cho
President, Bread for the World
Author, *Thou Shalt Not Be a Jerk: A Christian's Guide to Engaging Politics*

Introduction

Pastors, when was the last time you felt discouraged in ministry?

If you're honest, it might be right now. Or perhaps you can't even remember a time when you weren't carrying the weight of discouragement. Ministry is hard, and today, so many pastors are struggling with the realities of shepherding their congregations.

The struggle manifests in many forms. It can come through the pain of mistreatment—being disrespected or hurt by the very people you're called to love and lead. Whether it's abuse from parishioners or opposition from church leaders, the wounds cut deep. We pour our hearts into shepherding others, only to sometimes face betrayal or criticism. It's a path that eerily mirrors Jesus' own journey of being rejected and hurt by those He came to save. And while we might expect it, it doesn't make it any less painful.

For some pastors, the darkness arises from unhealed wounds of the past—pains we've buried deep but never truly dealt with. These unresolved hurts often lead us to suppress our emotions, masking our struggles behind a façade of strength or grandiosity. We strive to prove our worth, attempting to silence the shame and the relentless fear that we're not enough. Yet, this endless pursuit of success often leaves us drained and burned out. In our exhaustion, we may find ourselves turning to sinful addictions as a desperate and misguided attempt to find relief from the weight we carry.

Then there's the weight of feeling like a failure. Many pastors battle the daily reminder that no matter how hard they work, their churches aren't growing. They pour their time and energy into ministry, yet the numbers don't reflect their efforts. And sometimes, these voices of doubt and inadequacy are echoed by church leaders, reinforcing the idea that we're ineffective in our calling.

Ministry is an incredibly challenging journey, and if you're feeling its heavy weight, know that you're not alone. Many pastors today are grappling with burnout, struggling to keep going under immense pressure. Some have even reached the point of contemplating stepping away from ministry altogether. The burden is especially intense for senior pastors, who often feel isolated as they carry the responsibility of leading their congregations. The sacred calling God has placed on pastors' lives is being tested in ways we've never seen before.

According to the Barna Group, 42 percent of pastors considered leaving ministry altogether. The leading reasons cited include overwhelming job stress, feelings of isolation, and a deep sense of loneliness.[1] For senior pastors, the challenges are even more severe, with a staggering 18 percent—nearly one in five—admit to having struggled so deeply in ministry that they have contemplated suicide.[2] These statistics reveal a troubling reality about the mental and emotional toll of pastoral ministry.

This heartbreaking reality underscores the immense pressure and challenges that many pastors face as they strive to remain faithful to the calling God has entrusted to them. Ministry is undeniably challenging, and too often, pastors bear this weight in silence, feeling as though they must navigate these struggles on their own. Ministry is difficult, but you don't have to face it alone. There is hope, even in the struggle.

I wrote this book for pastors and church leaders who are wrestling with the challenges and struggles of ministry. For many, the burden feels overwhelming, leaving them wondering if they're doing something wrong or questioning their calling altogether. What if the root of the struggle isn't failure but a fundamental misunderstanding of how ministry is meant to be done?

What if we've been taught—or simply assumed—that ministry should operate the way the world measures success: through strengths, accomplishments, and self-sufficiency? But what if ministry was never meant to be built on our strengths? What if we embraced a completely different approach—a ministry philosophy rooted in weakness rather than strength?

Imagine what the church could look like if pastors and leaders stepped into their roles with a willingness to lead from their weaknesses rather than their strengths. What if vulnerability and authenticity became the foundation of our leadership? What if, instead of trying to gather people around our strengths, we found that it is our shared weaknesses that unite us and create space for God's transformative power?

This book is an invitation to reimagine ministry, not as a performance of perfection, but as an honest journey of faith where God's power is made perfect in our weakness. It's about discovering the freedom, hope, and strength that come when we embrace the counterintuitive truth that the heart of pastoral ministry is found not in our ability but in our dependence on Him.

My hope is that this book sparks a movement of weak churches, not just in the United States, but across the globe. I envision a world where pastors from every corner of the earth boldly lay down their reliance on personal strengths and embrace their weaknesses, allowing God's power to shine through their vulnerability. This is not just about changing the way we lead; it's about transforming the very culture of the church so that we can truly reach and connect with weak and broken people.

Too often, we've been led to believe that the way to reach the world is through projecting strength, competence, and success. But when did we start thinking that broken and hurting people could be reached through a display of our strengths? The truth is, people in pain are not drawn to perfection; they are drawn to authenticity. They need leaders who understand weakness, who have wrestled with their own humanity, and who can meet them where they are.

This book is a call to pastors to become weak pastors, leading weak churches that reflect the heart of the Gospel. My hope and prayer is that this book will be like living water for pastors and church leaders whose souls feel parched and weary. May *The Weak Church* become new wine, revitalizing both you and your congregation.

You will be challenged to lay down the masks of strength and step into the radical honesty of vulnerability. In doing so, we can create churches that serve as sanctuaries for the hurting, the lost, and the weary—places where God's grace is not just spoken but is tangibly felt and lived out in the very essence of the community.

My hope is that this movement becomes a global shift in how we view ministry, leadership, and the church itself. Weakness is not a liability in the Kingdom of God; it is the very place where His power is perfected. Together, as pastors and church leaders, we can build communities that embody this truth and lead countless others back to the healing and hope found in Jesus Christ.

The time to act is not later—it's now! Across the nation, young people are leaving the church in staggering numbers, particularly those from the Gen Z cohort. The latest data paints a sobering picture: over one million young people are walking away from the church every single year![3] This isn't just a trend; it's a crisis that threatens the future of the faith community as we know it.

The reasons behind this exodus are complex, but a recurring theme emerges: a disconnect between the church and the deep longing of young people for authenticity, vulnerability, and relevance. Many feel that the church is out of touch with their struggles or unwilling to address the real issues they face. For Gen Z, who have grown up in a world filled with uncertainty, polarization, and relentless pressure, the church's perceived inability to foster a genuine connection is pushing them away.

This crisis demands immediate and urgent attention. We can no longer afford to dismiss these alarming trends as temporary or assume they will resolve themselves. The time has come for a radical rethinking of how we approach every facet of ministry—preaching, discipleship, community building, and leadership.

What would it look like for the church to truly become a place where people feel seen, heard, and embraced? A sanctuary where their vulnerabilities are met with grace, and their questions are welcomed? Imagine a church culture where weakness reigns, where the brokenness of humanity is not hidden but brought into the light, allowing God's transformative power to work through it.

What kind of revival could happen if pastors, lay leaders, and church members alike practiced regular confession—not just privately to God but openly with one another, creating spaces of accountability, healing, and grace?

What kind of impact could be made if pastors used the pulpit not just to deliver polished sermons but to authentically share their own struggles with sin, doubts, and complexities of life? Could this vulnerability inspire and empower people in small groups to open up about their own struggles, fostering deeper connections?

How many more effective leaders could we raise up if leadership development moved away from the traditional classroom model and embraced a life-on-life approach? Imagine leaders being shaped not only by theological and theoretical lessons but also by walking alongside a pastor or church leader, learning through real-life experiences.

What if our compassion and service to the poor flowed from our own acknowledgment of spiritual poverty, reminding us that we are not "saviors" but servants walking alongside those in need?

Imagine a church that wholeheartedly embraces the truth that the Gospel extends beyond personal salvation to include justice—especially racial justice—and actively seeks to embody this truth in its ministries and relationships. Could the church become a living reflection of heaven itself, where people from every tribe, tongue, and nation come together in unity to worship Almighty God?

And what if the church staff became the living embodiment of this culture of weakness? What would happen if paid leaders of the church were intentionally trained to embrace their own weaknesses, setting the tone for the entire congregation? Staff who modeled this level of vulnerability would create a ripple effect, transforming the church into a place where weakness is no longer seen as a liability but as the very avenue through which God's strength is revealed.

The possibilities are endless, but the time for action is now. If we are willing to rethink our approach and embrace a ministry rooted in God's power perfected in our weakness, we may begin to see a church that not only retains its people but also becomes a beacon of hope for a generation longing for something real. Let us rise to the challenge and reimagine what the church can be.

I wish I could say that building a weak church was a task that came effortlessly, devoid of any substantial challenges. In truth, the journey of establishing a weak church stands as one of the most challenging yet profoundly rewarding undertakings I've ever engaged in. Over the span of two decades, Metro Community Church has served as my testing ground, a laboratory for ideas and concepts. The forthcoming pages capture years of bold experimentation, encompassing risks that would likely never cross the minds of most ministry leaders.

In the chapters ahead, we will confront the silent crisis of people leaving the church and delve into how our fixation on strength has permeated leadership and shaped church culture. We'll address how to break free from this obsession with strength by introducing and defining the concept of *weakology*. From there, we'll explore practical steps/principles to transform our congregation into a *Weak Church*—a community that speaks not only to the hearts of the younger generation but also to every generation.

The challenge before us is urgent. Millions are walking away from the church, and the time to address this crisis is now. Yet, within this urgency lies an extraordinary opportunity for transformation. Together, we can create weak churches that speak to the deepest needs of the human heart—a sanctuary for connection, healing, and hope in a fractured world. Let us seize this moment and take the steps needed to shape a church that reflects the heart of Christ.

Notes

1. Barna Group, "Pastors Share Top Reasons They've Considered Quitting Ministry in the Past Year," Barna. April 27, 2022, accessed December 2, 2024, https://www.barna.com/research/pastors-quitting-ministry/.

2. Barna Group, "Pastors, Too, Grapple with Thoughts of Suicide, Self Harm," Barna. September 12, 2024, accessed December 2, 2024, https://www.barna.com/research/pastors-thoughts-suicide-self-harm/.

3. Tenx10, "With 1 Million Leaving the Church Every Year, Is Gen Z the Faithless Generation?" Sojourners. February 26, 2024, accessed December 2, 2024, https://sojo.net/articles/sponsored/1-million-leaving-church-every-year-gen-z-faithless-generation.

~

CHAPTER 1

The Silent Crisis

Our Obsession with Strength

There is a silent crisis brewing within The Church. It's so subversive most congregations are oblivious to its ravenous power. The Barna Group and Pew Research Center have unearthed the undeniable truth: the steady decline in church attendance, a trend acutely visible among the Gen Z cohort. Year after year, Christians are exiting the church, while non-Christians hold no interest in the body where Jesus Christ serves as the head. While we can discern the effects of this silent crisis, we struggle to identify its origin or essence.

I grew up in a physically abusive home. My father wasn't necessarily an alcoholic, but when he did drink, it was with the intent to get drunk. He would often return home late, whether from work or a friend's house, struggling to insert the key into the worn, rustic wooden door, all while under the influence. The telltale sound of his key fumbling in the lock always signaled trouble.

Upon hearing that familiar struggle, my mother would quickly usher my two sisters and me into the bedroom, instructing us to hide beneath the bed. She didn't flee or seek refuge with us; instead, she remained in the living room, bracing herself each time he returned drunk, hoping to bear the brunt of her husband's anger. For years, my mother endured physical abuse at the hands of my father. She sacrificed her own physical well-being in a desperate attempt to protect her children. Unfortunately, her efforts were not always successful because, after he had finished assaulting her, my father would sometimes enter our bedrooms, reaching under the bed to drag us out, subjecting his three children to the remnants of his rage.

During my early years, my father was a monster. He was unable to express love for his family due to the deep-seated brokenness he had carried since his childhood in what is now North Korea during Japanese colonization. His mother had passed away when he was very young. While his father was intermittently detained in a camp, forcibly separated from his family by Japanese authorities, his stepmother subjected him to years of physical abuse. He was a man broken and unloved throughout his life, and these unhealed wounds led him to unleash his pain and frustrations on his own family when he became an adult.

I loathed my father. My hatred for him was matched only by my profound fear of him. Growing up, I never felt safe in his presence.

Regrettably, these were pivotal years of my development, marred by the trauma I endured in silence. The abuse I suffered remained a closely guarded secret, a topic never discussed within our family. We dared not share our agonizing truth with anyone, especially not within the church community.

I can't pinpoint precisely when my family first started attending church, but I do recall regularly attending services from my upbringing in Queens, NY. Even after our move to New Jersey during my third-grade year, my parents continued to make the Sunday trek back to Elmhurst, Queens, for church. At church, my parents assumed a different persona. They appeared to be the ideal, loving couple, concealing their pain and brokenness behind a spiritual facade. Early on, I realized that vulnerability had no place within our church community. It was a realm where we needed to project spiritual strength, even if it was far from authentic.

During my college years, I participated in a men's retreat organized by our church. Until then, I had never disclosed the truth about my abusive upbringing to anyone. Summoning all my courage, I tearfully shared my painful past during the retreat. However, the pastor's response was nothing short of disheartening. He stared at me for a few seconds, then swiftly moved on to the next participant to share. It was as if the gravity of my revelation held no significance. No one in that group approached me with words of support or encouragement. I left that experience feeling dispirited and wounded, vowing never to reveal my pain and struggles within the confines of the church again.

My college experience in the Church is unfortunately a very common one for those who are in a place of vulnerability or "weakness." When these individuals step into the Church, instead of feeling safe and accepted, they ultimately leave feeling looked down upon and marginalized. Even in the Church—or perhaps, especially in the church—people often feel the need to put up their guards for fear of judgment. Why does this happen?

The answer lies in the Church's tragic inability to distinguish itself from the world. The Church, instead of being a place that offers an alternative from the patterns of this broken world, has become another extension of the world in which it encourages its people to find their commonality in their strengths.

When individuals like myself enter a church with a broken past, their presence is often perceived as an inconvenience or interruption. When a society functions according to a norm defined by those who are *strong*, the society is said to promote strength. Not only that, but we naturally surround ourselves with people who have the same strengths as us. This is not just something that our culture teaches us, but it is how our brain is naturally wired.

The tendency to connect with one another based on our strengths has been supported by psychological studies of the human brain. It's been shown that our brains find their points of connection with others through characteristics that often mark our strengths. These traits include socioeconomic status, vocation, ethnicity, interests, and so on. Psychologist Dr. Thalia Wheatley uses the term "homophily," which is the idea that "like befriends like."[1]

Homophily describes how birds of a feather flock together, where the "feathers" are things like age, ethnicity, and education level: People tend to become friends with those of the same demographic characteristics. That raises the question of whether demographic traits cause particular neural patterns. If so, then similar brain-activity patterns in friends would simply be the result of people with similar education levels, ethnicities, and other traits—perhaps including ideological beliefs, recreational interests, and cultural preferences—gravitating toward one another. . . . Responding to the world in a similar way, as measured by brain activity, underlies the phenomenon of clicking: It's why you and that stranger at a party or assigned roommate laugh at the same things, want to chat endlessly about the same topic, and see the logic in the same argument. If two people interpret and respond to the world in similar ways, they're easily able to predict one another's thoughts and actions, Wheatley said. This increased predictability makes it easier to interact and communicate, which makes conversations and shared experiences more enjoyable. It also makes friendships more likely.[2]

On the flip side, those who are unable to "click" with others find it difficult to navigate social gatherings at church, work, and other contexts due to the inability of their brain's neural patterns to connect with other people's neural patterns. "People whose conversations with strangers and even acquaintances are riddled with awkward silences might have neural patterns that are out of sync with almost everyone else's. They don't find the same things interesting, their attention rarely lands where others' does, and as a result they don't click."[3]

With this understanding of how our society and brains function, the best anyone can do with respect to relating with those who are different from us is to tolerate them. This would also include those in the Church. When we tolerate someone, we are ultimately devaluing him or her. We don't see them as fully human, but rather, as lesser versions of us, and we can't help but look down on or feel superior to them, especially if we are in the majority. We cannot love them the way we have been called to love our neighbors because our strengths and neural patterns in our brain prohibit us from getting to fully know them.

Over the years, experts in church growth have attempted to tackle the persistent decline in church attendance by presenting solutions reminiscent of business strategies, aiming to enhance organization and appeal. With the right alpha leader this has worked for some congregations, but for the majority of churches, it has not. Unfortunately, many pastors now feel more insecure about their leadership because they were not able to grow their congregation. Attempting to heal a substantial wound with a mere Band-aid yields minimal results, and this parallels the efforts of church growth experts. Their intent was to provide church leaders and pastors with a superficial remedy for a much deeper affliction that plagues the church.

What exactly is the silent crisis haunting the church today? *It's none other than the church's inability to connect with and minister to people's weaknesses and struggles in life.* Pastors and church leaders often minister from a position of strength, creating a culture in which parishioners identify more with their strengths than their weaknesses. Just like the broader world, the church has become obsessed on the concept of strength. Our society places a premium on those who emerge as champions—individuals who achieve, conquer, and stand as the pinnacle of excellence. Think of the allure we find in figures like Shohei Ohtani, LeBron James, Serena Williams, Chloe Kim, Elon Musk, Jeff Bezos, Andy Stanley, Steve Furtick, Rick Warren, and Dave Ferguson. Our fascination with these winners is insatiable.

Consider when we step into a job interview. Our instinct is to project an image of competence and strength. Could you even fathom crafting a CV that openly acknowledges your weaknesses? The thought seems alien, foreign—largely because we inhabit a world where only the fittest survive. Gradually, this mindset has effected our spiritual outlook, convincing us that success hinges on unwavering strength.

What happened to me at that men's retreat is a microcosm of church practice throughout the world, regardless of ethnicity. If the church continues to minister out of its strength, ostracizing the weak and making them feel like spiritual and social outcasts, then their exodus from the church will be the new normal. This is the silent crisis that has pervaded the Church for centuries.

This crisis has now reached a crescendo. People, especially young people are leaving the church. While we once would say it was because of an age difference or personal preference to music or preaching, congregants and seekers alike are making the exodus.

According to Pew Research Center, the Church is on a steady decline. Less and less people are identifying with the Christian faith. "Sixty-five percent of American adults describe themselves as Christians when asked about their religion, down 12 percentage points over the past decade. Meanwhile, the religiously unaffiliated share of the population, consisting of people who describe their religious identity as atheist, agnostic, or 'nothing in particular,' now stands at 26 percent, up from 17 percent in 2009."[4] And as mentioned before, church attendance is also declining.

> Over the last decade, the share of Americans who say they attend religious services at least once or twice a month dropped by 7 percentage points, while the share who say they attend religious services less often (if at all) has risen by the same degree. In 2009, regular worship attenders (those who attend religious services at least once or twice a month) outnumbered those who attend services only occasionally or not at all by a 52%-to-47% margin. Today those figures are reversed; more Americans now say they attend religious services a few times a year or less (54%) than say they attend at least monthly (45%).[5]

According to Barna Research, the Gen Z cohort, which includes those born in the years 1999–2015, is even more unlikely to regularly attend church. "Gen Z grows less likely to regularly attend church and prioritize faith: 19 percent of 15-year-olds meet Barna's definition of practicing Christian, compared to just 9 percent of 19-year-olds."[6] One of the key characteristics that defines members of Generation Z is their openness in disclosing their inner lives. Growing up, these individuals were not only permitted to, but also highly encouraged to, explore their emotions and process them out loud in community. "Gen Z needs parents, pastors, teachers, and mentors who anticipate and prepare for deep, emotionally honest conversations."[7]

Research suggests that churches, as they stand, are not places in which people, especially young adults, can engage in *deep and emotionally honest conversations*. Young people are leaving "strong" churches because they are not finding them to be safe havens in which they are free to express their doubts and weaknesses.

Lifeway Research concluded that 66 percent of Christians between the ages of 18 and 22 stopped attending church for at least a year. In addition,

61 percent of Christian adults between the ages of 22 and 30 who leave the church say it was because their church seemed *judgmental or hypocritical* or that they struggled to connect with people in the church.[8]

Pastors and leaders must acknowledge that a church culture in which its congregants find their commonality in their strengths will often create second-class citizens out of the members who do not possess these same strengths. These individuals, in turn, are left feeling isolated and fearing judgment, and instead of attempting to find community within the church will leave instead. The church community is unable to love *the weak* fully and authentically the way we have been called to "love our neighbors" because, living in our strengths-oriented world, we no longer know how to meaningfully connect with those who exhibit vulnerability or weakness. And just to be absolutely clear, every person on this planet has weaknesses. No one is exempt from this truth. Nevertheless, somewhere in Church history congregations convinced themselves that our weaknesses should be concealed and locked up inside our souls, under a façade of unwavering strength, portraying a show of force in the presence of other people. We are always so ready to admit that we live in a broken and sinful world; yet, as pastors and church leaders, we are so unwilling to admit that we *are* broken and sinful people. This is precisely why the Church is unable to minister out of its weakness and allow the individuals within it to find their commonalities in their pain and struggles.

Before we can delve into the fundamental principles of a *Weak Church*, we must first establish the concept of "weakology." How does God perceive human weakness, and what advantage does God see when His church becomes vulnerable?

Notes

1. Sharon Besley, "Why You Click With Certain People," *Mind and Body*, August 16, 2018, accessed May 1, 2021, https://greatergood.berkeley.edu/article/item/why _you_click_with_certain_people.

2. Ibid.

3. Ibid.

4. Aleksandra Sandstrom, "In US, Decline of Christianity Continues at a Rapid Pace," *Pew Research Center*, October 17, 2019, accessed May 1, 2021, https://www .pewforum.org/2019/10/17/in-u-s-decline-of-christianity-continues-at-rapid-pace/.

5. Ibid.

6. Barna Group, Gen Z Volume 2, A Barna Report and Impact 360 Institute, 2021. 19.

7. Ibid., 9.

8. Lifeway Research, "Most Teenagers Drop Out Of Church When They Become Young Adults," *Lifeway Research*, January 15, 2019, accessed May 1, 2021, https://lifewayresearch.com/2019/01/15/most-teenagers-drop-out-of-church-as-young-adults/.

~

CHAPTER 2

Weakology

Theology of Weakness

Tommy, a dedicated veteran who had bravely served in the U.S. military, including the Gulf War, possessed numerous reasons to take pride in his accomplishments, or so I believed. Over the years, as he attended Metro, I had developed a strong fondness for him. As we drove together to grab a meal, I couldn't help but notice his admiration for some of the more luxurious and expensive cars on the road.

During our conversation, Tommy recounted an incident from a few weeks prior when he had encountered an old high school friend driving a Mercedes Benz. Rather than honking or attempting to get his old friend's attention, Tommy confessed that he instinctively lowered his head, even while driving, to avoid being noticed. He admitted that he felt inadequate compared to his friend's perceived success, simply because of the car he was driving—an old Toyota Camry.

In Tommy's eyes, his friend's possession of a luxurious car was equated with success, while his own lack of such a status symbol left him feeling inferior. It was a stark reminder of the judgments we often make based on superficial appearances, and the weight we assign to material possessions in defining success and power. Tommy's insecurities weighed heavily on him, to the point where he couldn't bring himself to greet a high school friend with whom he had lost touch for many years.

We live in a world where the demand to always be at our best is constant. This expectation entails projecting strength across diverse social scenarios. Finding moments of vulnerability amid this prevailing ethos is a rarity. For instance, within educational settings, students are assessed by their grades, perpetuating a culture of competition for excellence. Similarly, in professional environments, employees are expected to consistently deliver outstanding performance to impress superiors. Even within our social circles, the pressure to stand out, maintain a unique personality, and keep pace with the achievements of peers is palpable. And unfortunately, it is no different when we go to church.

Everywhere we turn, the expectation to exude strength prevails. Navigating through various situations, the burden to uphold this facade is relentless. Consequently, being weak becomes a daunting task in a world that predominantly values strength and power.

When was the last time you felt truly at ease with displaying your weakness? To embrace your genuine self without fear of judgment? In a society that reveres power and fortitude, the inclination to conceal weaknesses is ingrained. The constant toggling of the "strong switch" in public spaces can be exhausting, leaving little room for vulnerability.

This is why Tommy found himself concealing his insecurities from his high school friend. Feeling inadequate and intimidated by his friend's perceived strength, he resorted to masking his true self, evident even in the choice of vehicle they were driving.

God's Understanding of Human Weakness

God perceives human weakness differently than we do. Instead of shying away from weakness, the Almighty encourages His people to embrace it. Why? Does God take pleasure in seeing us downtrodden? Certainly not! Quite the contrary. For God, our weaknesses provide the perfect landscape for showcasing His power. Rather than relying on our own strength, God desires us to lean on His power and might. It is only when we acknowledge our weaknesses that we recognize our need for someone who is strong and mighty. And who better fits that description than God Himself?

Therefore, when churches avoid weakness and perpetuate a culture centered on strength and power, they inadvertently place themselves at a significant disadvantage. By neglecting to minister out of weakness, they operate in ministry without fully harnessing the perfect power of God, often leading to a state of spiritual impotence.

Jesus' words recorded in 2 Corinthians 12:9 provide the foundation for the Weak Church model: "My grace is sufficient for you, for my power is made perfect in weakness." In understanding this verse, Christian leaders and the people of God must acknowledge that God's grace is most powerfully at work in one's life when they are weak. The Apostle Paul's weakness was the thorn on his side. He had prayed fervently to God that it would be removed. Jesus did not remove this thorn, rather Jesus helped Paul to see the power of the thorn. Paul was so moved by this that he declared: "Therefore I will boast all the more gladly about my weaknesses, so that Christ's power may rest on me. That is why, for Christ's sake, I delight in weaknesses, in insults, in hardships, in persecutions, in difficulties. For when I am weak, then I am strong."[1] Pastors and church leaders must have this same posture as the Apostle Paul in which they naturally gravitate toward ministering out of their weakness rather than their strength. This is the only way through which Christians can minister with the full capacity of God's grace, power, and mercy. Peter Scazzero so beautifully writes that "when we live and build entire churches characterized by weakness and vulnerability, something inexplicable happens. People enjoy a taste of God's beauty and presence in Christ. A glimpse of the truth and the goodness of heaven shines. God's gentle power flows. People soften."[2]

The Church must embrace a ministry philosophy rooted in weakness to truly harness the power of God. Without this shift, the Church will perpetually fall short. A glaring deficiency in many modern churches is their failure to demonstrate God's power. While they excel in proclaiming the Gospel, they often lack the ability to manifest God's power as witnessed in the ministry of Jesus and his disciples.

The issue isn't with the proclamation of the Gospel; again many churches excel in this regard. Rather, the problem lies within the Church's inability to demonstrate God's power to their congregations. This isn't solely about charismatic practices like speaking in tongues or miraculous healings—though these can be valid demonstrations of divine power. Instead, it's about embracing what theologian Dr. Ray Anderson terms our "ex nihilo."

Anderson contends that ministry achieves its utmost potency when born from individuals' barrenness, their "ex nihilo," a Latin expression meaning "out of nothing." God's grace embodies His omnipotence. It not only extends forgiveness for sins but also illuminates His love and redemption for His people. Therefore, to undertake ministry and guide God's people, a substantial infusion of God's grace is imperative—it serves as the wellspring of divine power.

For Christians to access the purest manifestation of God's grace, Anderson believes, it must originate from their weakness, their "ex nihilo." "The grace of God must first kill before it can make alive. The grace of God requires barrenness, not our own belief, as a precondition."[3] Biblically speaking, there is a litany of stories in which God's grace is most powerfully demonstrated in people's barrenness.

When you examine the Bible from Genesis to Revelations, you will discover a theological thread that demonstrates how God's grace is most powerfully at work in our "ex nihilo." Why do you think God waited until Abraham was 100 years old and Sarah was in her nineties before they welcomed their promised child Isaac? Why did God choose Moses at a time in his life when he was a fugitive in his eighties with a speech impediment to lead his people out of Egypt? Why didn't God charge Moses to do this when he was in his twenties and living a comfortable life as part of the Egyptian royal family? Why did God call a young boy like David to go and fight the indomitable giant Goliath? Why did God instruct Gideon to downsize his army from 32,000 to a measly 300? Why did God choose a helpless thirteen-year-old virgin to give birth to the one and only Messiah? The answer to all of these questions is one and the same. In order for God's grace to be most powerfully at work, the element of human strength must first be completely destroyed.

If we genuinely seek to experience the most powerful manifestation of God's grace in our churches, it's imperative to acknowledge that God operates not through our strengths, but through our weaknesses and brokenness. *Therefore, being weak equates to being vulnerable.* A weak church is a vulnerable church where its members are willing to expose areas of their lives that make them feel weak. It's only when we can be completely honest and authentic with ourselves and the church community can we truly encounter God's perfect strength.

The church's embrace of weakness doesn't signify a defeatist mindset; rather, it signifies a deliberate choice to access the supernatural power of God, which is most potent when we acknowledge our vulnerability, our "ex nihilo." It's within this vulnerability that ministry can most effectively tap into the perfect power of God.

When we embrace vulnerability, we acknowledge our susceptibility to being "physically and emotionally wounded," as described by the Merriam-Webster dictionary. Contrary to popular belief, a weak church isn't synonymous with ineffectiveness; rather, it becomes supernaturally empowered in its ministry when pastors, leaders, and congregants minister with vulnerability, even at the risk of experiencing hurt. But how does vulnerability lead to being hurt?

Transparency versus Vulnerability

Transparency and vulnerability are often understood as synonyms, especially among younger individuals like those in the Gen Z cohort, who tend to prioritize transparency as a defining trait. Robin Emiliani of Catalyst Marketing Agency, an expert in helping companies connect with the Gen Z cohort, argues that the most effective way to reach them is through a marketing strategy centered on transparency. She emphasizes that "Gen Z values transparency, honesty, and real connections."[4] However, there's a crucial distinction between the two. While transparency involves openness, vulnerability goes a step further—it not only entails being open but also actively welcomes feedback. This nuanced difference highlights that transparency is merely the starting point, whereas vulnerability involves a willingness to receive feedback and grow from it.

It's this aspect of receiving feedback that exposes individuals to the possibility of being hurt. Therefore, when we opt for vulnerability, we willingly subject ourselves to potential hurt. However, despite the risks involved, the benefits of vulnerability outweigh the dangers because it opens the pathway to harnessing God's supernatural strength.

Unfortunately, the current Church often relies too heavily on human strength, resulting in ministry that lacks impact. Conversely, ministering from a place of weakness represents one of the purest forms of incarnational ministry. Just like God's brilliance and power is beautifully displayed through the birth of a weak baby Jesus, God also calls the church to weakness so that His power can radiate in and through us and transform the world.

Therefore, true holiness isn't determined by our actions or inactions; rather, it's defined by the extent of our vulnerability. By intentionally embracing vulnerability, we willingly place ourselves in a state of weakness, believing that it's in our weakness where God's power is most fully realized and perfected.

Today's youth often feel disillusioned by the church's failure to relate their lives to Jesus Christ. Instead of acknowledging our shared weaknesses, the church has embraced mainstream culture's emphasis on showcasing our strengths. However, these Christian strengths often alienate those outside the church.

For instance, while waking up at six in the morning to read the Bible may be commendable, it's not something that resonates with the broader world.

Conversely, if someone rises early to read the Bible as a means of coping with depression stemming from a history of abuse, both those within and outside the church can relate. Pain knows no boundaries—it affects people irrespective of ethnicity, gender, age, or socioeconomic status. In recognizing and sharing our vulnerabilities, we bridge the gap between the church and society, fostering genuine connections grounded in shared human experiences.

This is precisely why many marginalized individuals, often deemed weak by society, were irresistibly drawn to Jesus Christ. These outcasts found no acceptance among the Jewish religious leaders of Jesus' time, who frequently made them feel inferior. Instead, they were captivated by Jesus because He loved and embraced them not despite their weaknesses but because of them.

This is exemplified in Jesus boldly declaring Himself as the embodiment of Isaiah's prophecy in Luke 4:18–21: "The Spirit of the Lord is upon me, because he has anointed me to proclaim good news to the poor. He has sent me to proclaim freedom for the prisoners and recovery of sight for the blind, to set the oppressed free, to proclaim the year of the Lord's favor." Following this proclamation, Jesus rolled up the scroll, returned it to the attendant, and sat down. All eyes in the synagogue were fixed on Him as He declared, "Today, this scripture is fulfilled in your hearing."

I draw comfort from the connection I feel with Jesus' vulnerability, vividly portrayed in the Gospels. The truth is, none of us can genuinely comprehend Jesus' unyielding strength. As Paul wisely points out in Romans 3:23, we've all stumbled and fallen short of God's glory. Yet, what resonates universally is our ability to relate to Jesus' humanity—those moments of fragility and weakness that make Him profoundly relatable to each of us.

One story that profoundly speaks to me is the scene in the Garden of Gethsemane, where Jesus confides in his three closest disciples about the overwhelming anguish of his soul.[5] This raw display of Jesus' humanity serves as a source of immense comfort for me. Just like Him, I've faced moments in my life when the pain felt insurmountable, and death appeared as a preferable alternative.

Another deeply moving episode in Jesus' ministry occurred when he wept alongside Mary and Martha at the death of Lazarus, even though he knew he would soon raise Lazarus from the dead.[6] As a pastor, I've been honored to stand with many members of my congregation as they grieve the loss of loved ones. I understand that my role as a pastor isn't to provide them with a theological explanation for their suffering, but rather to offer a compassionate shoulder to cry on. While each loss carries its own weight, there are some that linger in my memory due to their especially tragic nature.

One such heartbreaking instance involved the death of a baby as a result of a tragic accident caused by a careless bus driver. I vividly recall receiving an urgent phone call from a family member, pleading for me to rush to the hospital because their eight-month-old baby had been fatally injured. The baby's mother was simply out for her daily walk when the unthinkable happened: a reckless bus driver collided with a metal pole, which tragically struck the baby's head, resulting in the baby's untimely death. The hours that followed, from that initial phone call to my arrival at the hospital, were undeniably the most agonizing moments of my entire pastoral career.

Upon meeting the grieving parents at the hospital, I found myself unable to offer any theological explanation for their profound loss. Instead, all I could do was weep alongside them, just as Jesus had wept with Mary and Martha. In that hospital room, there were no answers to provide, only tears to share. Our shared grief became a powerful expression of solidarity in the face of unimaginable pain and anguish. Through this experience, Jesus taught me the profound importance of mourning with those who mourn.

Another moment of Jesus' life that allows me to connect with him through his weakness is his crucifixion. Jesus was hanging on the cross, and as he was writhing in agony and pain, he didn't respond the way a superhero would. Instead, he responded in a way that is probably familiar to any one of us who has undergone hardships that seemed unbearable. Jesus cried out, "My God, my God, why have you forsaken me?"[7] There have been countless "low points" in my life, especially in relation to my father, when I truly felt that God had forsaken me. But a powerful thing happens in our lives when we find we can relate to Jesus' brokenness. We realize that Jesus understands our brokenness because he was broken too. We don't worship a distant God who sits up in heaven and listens to our cries, only to be unable to truly relate or empathize with what we are going through. Our God understands us and weeps for us because God, also, was broken many times—literally and figuratively—when God entered into human history 2,000 years ago.

Jesus gravitated toward the most broken sinners and social outcasts of his time. They were drawn to him because, unlike the Jewish leaders, Jesus invested time in them, empathized with their weaknesses, and took the initiative to build relationships with them.

The Story of Zacchaeus

Zacchaeus was a wealthy tax collector. He was notorious for stealing people's money by inflating their taxes to the Roman government. Though he was wealthy, he was regarded and treated by the Jewish people and its leaders as a spectacular sinner. Therefore, he was a social outcast and even his money couldn't buy him any street credibility. People frequently looked down upon him and judged him for being a legalized thief.

One day, he heard that Jesus was in town and noticed much commotion stirring. People were rushing to catch a glimpse of Jesus and his powerful ministry. The mob of people made it impossible for Zacchaeus to even catch a quick look at this young spiritual celebrity. It sure didn't help that Zacchaeus was vertically challenged, but to add insult to injury, the people would not let Zacchaeus approach the front, or even crack a little passageway for him to catch a glimpse of Jesus. They judged him as a notorious sinner, and sinners such as Zacchaeus had no place in the front row. His place was in the back, and the human barricade was a painful reminder of his struggle to find any human support. Zacchaeus did not put up a fight. Rather, he became resourceful and climbed up a tree and watched Jesus teach and minister to the people from up above. When Jesus saw Zacchaeus, he invited himself to his house for dinner. This was indeed a strange and controversial request. In the Jewish culture, rabbis did not associate with, nor would they ever consider eating a meal with, a sinner like Zacchaeus. The first-century Jews found their commonality in their strengths, not in their weakness. This was especially true of the Pharisees, High Priests, and Sadducees—the trifecta of Jewish piety. To eat with a sinner like Zacchaeus meant that Jesus would open himself up for judgment through which his credibility as a rabbi would be in question. Zacchaeus knew all too well how bold and risky it was for Jesus to have dinner with him. But the rich tax collector didn't dwell on it for very long because of his elation of finally finding his human support in Jesus. As a result of being deeply moved by Jesus' love gesture, Zacchaeus promised the Son of God that he would give half of his wealth to the poor, and refund four times the amount he had taken from overtaxing people. Jesus boldly declared salvation for Zacchaeus.[8]

Why was Jesus able to embrace and love one of the greatest sinners of his generation? Because Jesus, though being God, had firsthand experience with poverty, socioeconomic hierarchies, social outcast, betrayal, and persecution, and he used his understanding of these narratives to relate to those to whom he reached out.

I wonder how people outside the church would respond to Christians relating to them out of the narrative of their own pain and brokenness. Would they flock to the church with the kind of intensity that Zacchaeus had when he climbed up that tree? And would a similar response like Zacchaeus become more the norm, rather than the exception?

The Story of My Sister Susan

When my sister Susan was a little girl, she was the most spiritual one in my family. She would remind our family that we needed to pray before every meal to thank God for His blessing. My parents would often marvel at the maturity of her spirituality that was so beyond her years. However, as she got older, her learning disability became more noticeable. She eventually left the Church and walked away from her faith. Why? It was because the Church was unable to accept her disabilities and fully embrace who she was. Instead, the Church community merely appeared to tolerate her, at best, or ignore her presence completely, at its worst. This inability to accept people who we deemed were "different" was so prevalent in our church culture that even I, her own brother, became complicit in ultimately leading her to feel like an outcast.

Sunday mornings often brought a sense of relief when Susan announced to our parents that she wouldn't be attending church. My sister Susan had a tendency to embarrass me, especially when the youth pastor called on her to read from the Bible. Her struggles with reading aloud left me anxious that others might link her learning disability to me, triggering feelings of shame. This shame silently pushed me to support her decision to skip church, fearing that her perceived weaknesses would somehow tarnish my image. Thus, when she disclosed her intentions to our parents, it felt like a burden had been lifted from my shoulders. Regrettably, I too bear responsibility for Susan's departure from Christianity.

It wasn't until I found myself in seminary, crafting a paper for a Family Therapy class, that this realization truly dawned on me. The assignment was to delve into the spiritual journey of each member of my nuclear family. I meticulously chronicled the paths of my father, mother, and my two older sisters, Ellen and Susan. However, when I reached the section about Susan, something stirred within me.

Susan's story brought back painful memories of how the church had overlooked her because of her disability. At best, they merely tolerated her attempts to connect with the girls in the youth group. My anger toward the church for its rejection of her surged within me. In the midst of this turmoil, God unveiled a truth that shattered me: I was complicit in Susan's separation from Christianity.

The weight of this revelation drove me to tears in the library. I rushed outside to call Susan and beg for her forgiveness. Through my tears, I assured her that both my rejection and the church's treatment of her didn't reflect the profound love God holds for her. Although her response was hesitant, she forgave me, saying, "Peter, of course I forgive you. I love you."

As I hung up the phone, a vision unfolded before me—a vision of Metro Community Church. It would be a sanctuary for souls like Susan, a place where those with disabilities could find belonging. At a weak church, someone like Susan, with her learning disability, could forge deep connections, even with those who had graduated from Ivy League schools. In a weak church, she wouldn't merely be tolerated; she'd be embraced, loved, and empowered to serve and lead ministries.

Isn't this the essence of the Kingdom of God? Shouldn't the church be a refuge where the weak can taste the boundless grace and love of Jesus Christ? But for this to happen, the church must adopt a ministry philosophy rooted in weakness, not strength.

Within and beyond the walls of the church, countless people yearn for a transformative encounter with the profound love and grace of God. As leaders within the church, we must embrace vulnerability in our leadership. Failure to do so not only hinders the work of God within our congregations but also restricts the boundless potential of His power.

Leading from a position of strength may seem more comfortable, allowing us to shield ourselves behind our perceived capabilities. However, true leadership demands the audacity to lead from a place of vulnerability—a task that requires unwavering courage. This path is not for the faint-hearted, but without it, we cannot authentically proclaim that "the Kingdom of God has come." Jesus Himself emphasized this truth, heralding the arrival of God's Kingdom, which finds its most potent manifestation in our weakness. Let us embrace our weaknesses without reservation.

Becoming a vulnerable leader is a herculean challenge. Many of us have journeyed through life without fully processing the wounds we've endured. Before delving into the nuts and bolts of a weak church, we must prioritize the emotional well-being of pastors and church leaders. Unless pastors and church leaders are emotionally healthy, they have no other choice but to abstain from being vulnerable as they minister to people.

The forthcoming chapter will outline the steps toward cultivating emotional health among leaders, laying the groundwork for the establishment of a weak church.

Notes

1. 2 Corinthians 12:9b–10.

2. Peter Scazzero, *Emotionally Healthy Discipleship* (Grand Rapids: Zondervan Reflective, 2021), 189.

3. Ray S. Anderson, *The Soul of Ministry* (Louisville: Westminster John Knox Press, 1997), 47.

4. Robin Emiliani, "Keeping it Real: Gen Z's Hunger for Authentic Marketing and Purpose Driven Brands," *Catalyst*, January 22, 2023, accessed September 9, 2024,

https://catalystmarketing.io/blog/gen-zs-hunger-for-authentic-marketing-and-pur pose-driven-brands/.

<ol start="5">
<li>Matthew 26:36–46.</li>
<li>John 11:17–44.</li>
<li>Mark 15:34.</li>
<li>Luke 19:1–10.</li>
</ol>

THE EIGHT PRINCIPLES
OF A WEAK CHURCH

~

CHAPTER 3

Why Emotional Health Matters in a Weak Church

Church planters are often viewed as the Navy SEALs among pastors, tasked by God with an improbable mission: to establish a church from scratch. It takes a particular brand of audacity to embark on such a venture, rallying a small group of believers with no guarantee of survival. Statistics show that most church plants will fail. Jeff Hoglen, a church planting consultant and editor, argues that "50%–80% of church plants will close within the first five years."[1] Only a handful manage to blossom into flourishing congregations.

Unlike Navy SEALs, who undergo intense and rigorous training, church planters often step into the field with little preparation for the challenges ahead. They may assume that having faith alone is enough to face the battles of church planting.

Church planting may seem appealing from the outside, but the reality is anything but glamorous. Once they begin, church planters soon face the harsh challenges and hard work involved, revealing the true nature of the journey.

On April 4, 2004, I founded Metro Community Church shortly after graduating from Fuller Theological Seminary in Pasadena, CA. Following graduation, I felt a clear calling from God to return to my roots in New Jersey, where my wife Jenny and I grew up, and plant Metro Community Church. Truth be told, I embarked on this journey with a profound sense of uncertainty. With no prior pastoral experience and being a second-career pastor, I found myself stepping into unfamiliar territory. But what I lacked in experience, I compensated for with bold and audacious faith.

As I worked to assemble the core team, I shared the vision of Metro Community Church with around sixty-five young individuals—friends, family, and former churchmates. Among them, only eleven chose to join me in launching what seemed like a fledgling endeavor. Within that small group of eleven was my wife, who had little choice but to support me, and my brother-in-law, Won. Feeling sympathy for our modest beginnings, Won, despite not identifying as a Christian at the time, decided to lend his support to our cause simply because of our familial ties. While it's typically preferable for core team members to share a belief in Jesus Christ, given our team's diminutive size, I didn't turn him away. He told me, "Peter, when the church reaches fifty people, I'm out of here." More than two decades later, as our congregation far exceeds fifty members, my brother-in-law, Won, still remains at Metro Community Church. He embraced Christianity around our second or third year of the church, and I had the honor of baptizing him.

Church or denominational leaders often fail to address the issue of our inclination toward grandiosity as church planters. We are drawn to the allure of exponential growth, sometimes to the extent that it becomes an idol in our hearts. While there's nothing inherently wrong with desiring church growth, when this ambition eclipses our desire for God, our ministry can veer off course. Instead of serving Jesus Christ, our actions become self-serving. Consequently, we become consumed with aspirations of expanding our churches into the hundreds, thousands, and in some cases, tens of thousands.

To be completely honest, my aspirations for Metro Community Church exceeded even those numbers. I dreamed of it becoming the largest church globally, with over a million attendees every Sunday. In my mind, the size of the church equated to the magnitude of my faith. I was driven by a fear of being labeled as someone lacking in faith by God. It was an audacious vision, driven by boundless grandiosity. What I failed to realize at the time was that this desire to attain the title of the world's largest church stemmed from my own emotional insecurities and unhealthiness.

The initial five years of Metro Community Church proved to be exceptionally challenging. Despite my efforts, I struggled to grow the congregation beyond 150 people, leaving me feeling deeply inadequate and like a failure. How could I ever fulfill my grand vision of making it the largest church in the world if I couldn't even surpass this modest milestone?

To cope with the overwhelming sense of shame and self-doubt, I began to seek solace by speaking at various churches, conferences, and retreats across the country. Speaking outside the confines of Metro Community Church provided temporary relief from the relentless inner voice that taunted me with accusations of failure. On average, I found myself traveling twice a month, leaving my wife, Jenny, to shoulder the responsibility of caring for our three young children virtually on her own. In essence, she became a single mother, bravely enduring the challenges without complaint, determined not to impede my perceived calling from God.

Unbeknownst to me at the time, Jenny bore the brunt of my relentless pursuit of success, suffering in silence as I grappled with my own insecurities and failures. My inability to confront these negative emotions left me oblivious to the toll it took on her.

Encountering other pastors for the first time always filled me with anxiety. It seemed inevitable that upon revealing my role as a church planter, the immediate question would be, "How many people attend your church?" For some inexplicable reason, I found myself inflating our numbers in response, adding a few extra dozens of attendees to our actual count. Although we were realistically averaging around 150 people, I would often claim 175 attendees at Metro weekly. Reflecting on this now, I can't help but shake my head. What difference would an extra twenty-five people really make? If I was going to bend the truth, why not go all the way and claim an attendance of 250? Yet, strangely, embellishing our numbers didn't quite feel like a lie to me; it felt more like a hopeful projection toward a future reality.

By the fifth year, I found myself utterly depleted and burned out. There was simply nothing left in me to offer. I vividly recall a leadership retreat I was tasked with leading for those I was discipling at Metro. It was a three-day retreat nestled in the Pocono Mountains of Pennsylvania. Frankly, I didn't want to attend. Exhaustion had taken its toll, leaving me feeling empty-handed. However, to my surprise, God's presence showed up at the retreat, and the attendees were deeply impacted. Yet, despite witnessing these blessings, I couldn't shake off my weariness. All I could think about was whether I had the strength to persevere. My exhaustion had peaked. Nevertheless, I knew I had to press on without ceasing. After all, there was a church to build, and in that pursuit, my personal feelings seemed inconsequential.

Saturday night was truly memorable; we engaged in the profound act of foot-washing and exchanged heartfelt affirmations within our leadership group. Over the past six months, this group had forged strong bonds, and witnessing their unity was deeply gratifying. I felt a profound sense of gratitude to God for allowing me to play a part in fostering this connection. As the night wore on, we retired to bed late, savoring every moment of the final night of the retreat.

With only about two hours of sleep, I woke up at 3 a.m. on Sunday morning to put the finishing touches on my sermon. By 5 a.m., I was on the road, determined to arrive at the church by 7 a.m. As a part of our portable church setup team, I was involved in arranging the space before delivering sermons at both the 9:30 a.m. and 11:30 a.m. services. After a brief respite at home for a hurried meal, I hosted newcomers from our church for our Newcomer's Connection Dinner at 4 p.m. Here, I shared the church's story, vision, and values before sharing a meal together. The event concluded around 7:30 p.m. Following a short 15-minute rest, I proceeded to my office for a counseling session with a married couple at 8 p.m. Exiting my office around 10:30 p.m., as I made my way to the parking lot, I found myself uttering these startling words: "I want to die." The realization of expressing such a sentiment shook me to my core, but it reflected the bleak state of my heart and life. The role of pastor, once a source of joy, had transformed into an overwhelming burden.

The elders of the church observed the toll that my deteriorating emotional health was taking on me; they could see that I was burning out. Out of genuine concern for my well-being, they made the decision that I needed to take a sabbatical. Initially, I adamantly refused, expressing my fears that stepping away from Metro would severely impact the church, especially given ongoing staffing issues. However, the elders remained resolute in their decision. They made it clear that this was not a suggestion but an order: I had to take a sabbatical. Reluctantly, and with much protest, I acquiesced. Thus, despite my protests and reluctance, I was compelled to step away from Metro Community Church for the next three months.

During the first month, I experienced what felt like a ministry detox—an uncomfortable and disorienting period. I found myself at a loss, unsure of how to occupy my time without the familiar rhythm of church duties. The longing to return to church and resume serving was palpable, but I understood the seriousness of the elders' directive.

In the second month, I began to explore various churches in the New York/New Jersey area. One particular Sunday, I attended New Life Fellowship Church in Elmhurst, Queens, hoping to hear Peter Scazzero preach. Much to my disappointment, I learned that he too was on sabbatical. Despite this setback, after the service, I noticed they were selling Peter Scazzero's books. Intrigued by the title, I decided to purchase, *Emotionally Healthy Spirituality* (EHS), even though I was unsure of its content.

As I delved into EHS, the words leapt from the pages and resonated deeply within me. It felt as though Peter Scazzero had penned this book specifically for me. Through its pages, I confronted the stark reality of my emotional unhealthiness and its detrimental impact on my relationship with God, my wife, and myself.

In this profound journey of self-discovery, I unearthed a sobering truth about pastors, particularly church planters: *our greatest temptations often revolve not around the things we lust after, but rather our greatest temptation is the desire to want to be spiritually lusted after*. We yearn for the admiration and reverence of others, desiring to be revered as spiritual authorities. We aspire to write books, deliver sermons at conferences worldwide, and bask in the admiration of countless admirers. It's a temptation rooted in the desire for spiritual lust directed toward us.

For me, achieving this spiritual lust hinged on transforming Metro Community Church into a mega-church. EHS served as a catalyst, enabling me to confront and grapple with this uncomfortable yet profoundly enlightening truth.

It's one thing to be open and transparent about your past struggles, but it's another to confront and acknowledge vulnerabilities in the present moment. I had to confront the harsh reality that my emotional struggles were not only hindering but actively harming Metro Community Church. At the core of this issue was the deep-seated shame that I grappled with daily. I will delve further into the topic of shame in the following chapter.

The trauma and emotional turmoil from my upbringing had never been addressed in my life. I never sought counseling or support to navigate and heal from the wounds I endured as a child. I was oblivious to the profound impact it had on every aspect of my life—as an adult, husband, father, son, and pastor.

Upon my return from sabbatical, I made a solemn vow to both myself and to God. I committed to living an unhurried life, embracing a contemplative spirituality, and seeking guidance from a professional counselor to address and unravel my past. This decision sparked a profound transformation in both my personal life and in the life of Metro Community Church.

If you're a pastor or church leader who has grown up in a dysfunctional family or experienced trauma, I cannot recommend seeking professional counseling highly enough. A mentor of mine once described counseling as "an emotional spa," and I've found this to be profoundly true. Over the past fifteen years of counseling, I've become a student of my own life, gaining invaluable self-awareness and uncovering emotional hang-ups that previously went unchecked. Before counseling, I was trapped in self-destructive patterns with no other option but to repeat them. Counseling has empowered me to recognize and break those toxic behaviors, giving me the power to make conscious choices about my actions. The ability to choose, whether to say "yes" or "no" to destructive patterns, is something I once underestimated. Thanks to self-discovery through counseling, I now have the power to choose a healthier path and avoid repeating past mistakes.

Why Emotionally Healthy Leaders Are Essential for a Weak Church

For a church to embrace weakness, its leaders must be willing to be vulnerable. Yet, achieving vulnerability becomes challenging when individuals grapple with emotional unhealthiness. This emotional instability can spread like a cancer, corroding not just spiritual well-being but also physical health.

Peter Scazzero, renowned for his groundbreaking work in *Emotionally Healthy Spirituality*, has dedicated his life to assisting Christians worldwide in achieving emotional wellness. He emphasizes that true spiritual health is unattainable without first achieving emotional health. Scazzero warns that neglecting emotional health within Christian spirituality can lead to detrimental consequences—for oneself, one's relationship with God, and for those around them. He writes, "Christian spirituality, without an integration of emotional health, can be deadly—to yourself, your relationship with God, and the people around you."[2]

To embrace a philosophy of weakness in ministry, pastors and church leaders must first prioritize their own emotional health as a central aspect of their discipleship. After all, the pace set by leaders often becomes the pace of the entire team. Therefore, it's essential for pastors and church leaders to prioritize their own emotional well-being before attempting to integrate it into the church's practices.

Once pastors and church leaders have embarked on their own journey toward emotional health, they can then integrate emotionally healthy spirituality into the church's discipleship model. Without this integration, there's a risk of the church reducing discipleship to a superficial exercise focused solely on intellectual stimulation, thus neglecting the profound matters of the heart.

Amy Volstad contends that it is possible for one to be spiritual but not emotionally healthy. In fact, she writes that people can use their spirituality to hide their emotionally unhealthy tendencies. In her experience as a counselor, she has counseled pastors and church leaders who were gifted in ministry and who were able to make significant contributions to the church with their leadership. Nevertheless, she writes that these pastors and church leaders struggle to be in healthy relationships with their family. "I know many spiritually powerful people who don't process emotions and can't be honest with their own struggles or pain. . . . Emotions have gotten a bad rap. They are not bad. God created emotions as ways to process what is happening inside of us. They are actually what makes us human and alive. Have you ever seen an emotionally dead person? It is heartbreaking."[3] Volstad writes that, in order for one to be emotionally healthy, these individuals need to take an honest look at themselves. "It has been said that only those who can communicate honestly with themselves can communicate honestly with others. We call that 'congruence' in psychology. What is happening on the inside of me is the same as what I am presenting on the outside of me."[4]

When a congregation disciples their people to become more emotionally healthy, they will naturally seek each other out and be vulnerable. Individuals cannot be vulnerable or weak unless they are emotionally healthy. Rabbi Dov Heller writes about the *Eight Habits of Emotionally Healthy People*. He stresses that vulnerability cannot exist outside of an emotionally healthy person. "Emotionally healthy people are not ashamed to be vulnerable and admit that they are in pain and need help. They let others in and are not afraid to lower their protective walls. They know the difference between normal life pain and suffering and have sufficient self-esteem to choose not to suffer."[5] Rabbi Heller argues that emotionally healthy people know how to reach out to people when they are struggling or need help rather than suffer alone.

In a Weak Church, there is a unique opportunity for emotional health to be intricately woven into the very fabric of its discipleship. When a church embraces a ministry philosophy that values vulnerability, it creates a nurturing environment where emotional health can flourish. Conversely, if a church lacks this commitment to vulnerability, its pastors and leaders may inadvertently sidestep the crucial aspect of emotional health being integral to our discipleship. Without a deliberate focus on creating spaces for the caring of our soul, emotional health becomes something that remains on the periphery, rather than being deeply integrated into the spiritual journey of its members.

Therefore, we will label a church that avoids embracing weakness as a "Strong Church." In this context, a Strong Church is a community centered around its collective strengths, reflecting the worldly emphasis on achievement and success. This focus on strength can cultivate an elitist culture that permeates every aspect of its leadership and ministry, resulting in an environment where only those who meet specific standards are valued, and where vulnerability is overlooked.

In a Strong Church, discipleship often centers on head knowledge—through inductive Bible studies, theology classes, and reading Christian books. While these practices are valuable, knowledge alone cannot lead us to truly follow Jesus Christ. As the Apostle Paul reminds us, "knowledge puffs up, while love builds up."[6] The true aim of discipleship is to enable Christians to love others well. However, a church cannot effectively guide its members in loving others unless it prioritizes the emotional health of its congregation. Our capacity to love is deeply intertwined with our emotional well-being. In Strong Churches, where the focus is primarily on intellectual understanding, members may find themselves ill-prepared to genuinely love, especially those they consider enemies.

In addition, Strong Churches often foster an environment in which individuals feel the need to compensate for their emotional unhealth by taking on more tasks and roles to appear "spiritual." The emotional unhealth of the church prevents them from becoming aware of and working through their own weaknesses and brokenness. Furthermore, as these individuals are unable to embrace their own weaknesses, they are also rendered useless in ministry to others who are weak and broken. Scazzero argues that the most current discipleship models often add an extra layer of protection against emotional maturity. Because people are experiencing real and helpful spiritual encounters through worship, prayer, Bible studies, and fellowship, they mistakenly believe that they are doing "fine," despite the disarray in their interior world. This apparent "progress" then provides a spiritual reason for not doing the hard work of maturing.[7]

So many people struggle today, suppressing their emotions, feeling like failures, being overwhelmed with the stresses of life, and not being true to themselves. These are all characteristics of emotionally unhealthy people, according to Michal Mitchell. Mitchell argues that our emotional well-being is more important than ever before. If we do not express our emotions naturally and continue suppressing them, they will build up. "Just because you consciously suppress your emotions, does not mean they go away. Instead, they build up. You should instead express emotions such as sadness, anger, or anxiety to someone you trust. Just imagine what could happen if you don't allow yourself to release an emotion like anger, and instead let it build up?"[8] A Strong Church doesn't help people deal with their emotions. As a result, people will not be discipled properly because emotional health is so deeply connected to spiritual health. The best these churches can hope for is a shallow Christianity.

In a Weak Church, the pastors, leaders, and members of the church have gone through the difficult work of becoming emotionally healthy. This allows them to be in touch with their limits, their patterns, and ultimately, their own brokenness and vulnerability. Because they see themselves accurately and fully, they can relate and minister powerfully to others out of their weakness.[9] The Church is most effective in ministering to people inside and outside of its walls when it stops offering theological answers, and instead, offers a shoulder to cry on. In a Weak Church, people are able to spiritually thrive, even when faced with trials and difficult seasons in their lives, because they have done the hard work of digging beneath the surface of their souls.

Christians sometimes deny the emotions that they feel because they believe that emotions are not spiritual or holy. Contrary to this belief, our emotions are an essential part of what makes us human. Jesus is the perfect example of how Christians must engage with their emotions. Throughout the gospels, Jesus experienced a full range of emotions, just as people do. The Bible states that "For this reason he had to be made like them, fully human in every way, in order that he might become a merciful and faithful high priest in service to God, and that he might make atonement for the sins of the people."[10] "For we do not have a high priest who is unable to empathize with our weaknesses, but we have one who has been tempted in every way, just as we are—yet he did not sin."[11] The famous theologian John Calvin made a powerful statement when he declared that "the Son of God having clothed himself with our flesh, of his own accord clothed himself also with human feelings, so that he did not differ at all from his brethren, sin only excepted."[12] Before the fall of Adam and Eve, their emotions were completely healthy and in line with God. We would cease to be fully human, created in the image of God, if we did not embrace our emotions fully. What does a Godly and emotional life look like? Jesus was the perfect model of an emotionally healthy person. He got angry and showed compassion. He was able to fully understand the emotions of life as he, too, lived them for thirty-three years.

For a church to become "weak," its leaders and people must grow in emotional health. Emotionally unhealthy individuals pose a risk to the church. Furthermore, emotionally unhealthy pastors and leaders become enormous liabilities to the church. In *Emotionally Healthy Leader*, Scazzero integrates a leader's inner spiritual life to core leadership tasks such as planning, decision-making, team-building, setting boundaries, navigating dual relationships, exercising power, and embracing endings for new beginnings. He makes a bold claim that "the emotionally unhealthy leader is someone who operates in a continuous state of emotional and spiritual deficit, lacking emotional maturity and 'being with God' sufficient to sustain their 'doing for God.'"[13] As a result, the leader lacks the self-awareness to enter deeply into the feelings and perspectives of others, which compromises their leadership.

The most effective way the church and its leaders can grow in emotional health is to offer Peter Scazzero's *Emotionally Healthy Spirituality* course. In this study, people learn to delve beneath the surface of their souls. The topics include:

1. *The Problem of Emotionally Unhealthy Spirituality*
2. *Know Yourself that You May Know God*
3. *Going Back in Order to Go Forward*
4. *Journeying through the Wall*
5. *Enlarge Your Soul through Grief and Loss*
6. *Discover the Rhythms of Daily Office and Sabbath*
7. *Grow into an Emotionally Mature Adult*
8. *Develop a "Rule of Life"*

This eight-week course challenges people in the church to grow in emotional health, which, in turn, leads them to embrace the ministry philosophy of being "weak." Unless the church is growing in emotional health, it will continue to be a community that relies on strengths to find commonality with one another. Our emotional health is deeply connected to our spiritual health. The more emotionally healthy we are, the more we can love in healthy ways. Peter Scazzero contends that emotionally healthy adults

- are able to ask for what they need, want, or prefer—clearly, directly, honestly;
- recognize, manage, and take responsibility for their own thoughts and feelings;
- can, when under stress, state their own beliefs and values without becoming adversarial;
- respect others without having to change them;
- give people room to make mistakes and not be perfect;
- appreciate people for who they are—the good, bad, and ugly—not for what they give back;
- accurately assess their own limits, strengths, and weaknesses and are able to freely discuss them with others;
- are deeply in tune with their own emotional world and able to enter into the feelings, needs, and concerns of others without losing themselves; and
- have the capacity to resolve conflict maturely and negotiate solutions that consider the perspectives of others.[14]

Emotionally mature adults are self-aware and are comfortable in who they are. This allows them to be vulnerable. If a church does not develop its people to become emotionally healthy, it will be unable to function as a Weak Church.

The Nuts and Bolts of Integrating Emotional Health into Discipleship

Once a year, Metro Community Church offers a sixteen-week "Emotionally Healthy Discipleship Course," divided into two eight-week workshops. The first workshop focuses on Emotionally Healthy Spirituality (EHS), while the second workshop delves into Emotionally Healthy Relationships. For further details, please visit their website: www.emotionallyhealthy.org.

"Emotionally Healthy Discipleship Course" stands as a fundamental pillar of spiritual formation at Metro Community Church. Prospective members are required to complete the EHS workshop or commit to doing so within twelve months of becoming members of the church. This policy underscores the belief of Metro's leadership that emotional health is essential for individuals to effectively contribute to and uphold the ethos of the "Weak Church" ministry philosophy.

In addition to the sixteen-week "Emotionally Healthy Discipleship Course," Metro also provides workshops designed to train and equip our congregation in emotional health within the contexts of marriage and parenting. It's important to reflect on how often we've faced challenges in our marriages and parenting due to a lack of emotional health. Many of us can recall moments where our responses were driven more by emotional instability than by thoughtful consideration, leading to misunderstandings, hurt, and conflict.

I firmly believe that to truly embody emotional health in the church, we must first nurture it within our homes. Only then can we authentically model this vital aspect of discipleship in our church community. Through these workshops, we aim to guide our congregation on a transformative journey toward becoming emotionally mature adults. This process starts at home, where relationships are nurtured and developed, and extends into the church, allowing us to create a supportive and understanding environment for one another.

The goal is not just to improve individual relationships, but to foster a community rooted in emotional health, ultimately strengthening and empowering our entire church family to embrace their weaknesses.

John, a long-standing member of Metro Community Church and a successful businessman, requested a lunch meeting with me to discuss his decision to leave the church. I was taken aback by his announcement and asked him to elaborate on his reasoning. John explained that he and his wife were departing because of their disagreement with EHS, believing it to be non-biblical and a diversion from the core teachings of the Bible. Despite my efforts to persuade him otherwise, he remained steadfast in his stance.

Upon further conversation and learning more about John's past, I realized that his aversion to EHS stemmed from his reluctance to confront and process his own history—a crucial aspect of the EHS course. Throughout his life, John had suppressed his past, avoiding acknowledgment of the challenging seasons he had endured. Despite his success in his vocation and his esteemed reputation within the church as a knowledgeable Bible teacher, John feared the repercussions of delving into his unresolved emotions. The prospect of revisiting his past and unlocking the Pandora's box of suppressed feelings was simply too daunting for him to bear.

The fear of confronting the unknown depths of our souls often paralyzes many Christians today. Instead of facing the painful realities of rejection, loss, and past wounds, we prefer to hide behind a facade of spirituality and showcase our knowledge of the Bible.

Where do you stand? Are you willing to embark on the journey toward becoming an emotionally healthy adult? This journey is lifelong—a path I embarked on over fifteen years ago, and it has allowed me to deepen my relationship with God in ways I never thought possible.

No longer driven by the ambition to grow Metro Community Church into a mega-church—a seven-digit church—I now embrace myself fully, with all my limitations and the gifts given to me by God. Metro stands as a Weak Church, leading from a place of vulnerability. Had I not undertaken this journey toward emotional health fifteen years ago, I wouldn't be serving as a pastor today.

I can honestly say that I find greater fulfillment in being a child of God, a husband, and a father than in being a pastor. This shift is a testament to my emotional health and spiritual growth.

But I wish I could tell you that the journey toward emotional health was all smooth sailing. Unfortunately, it's far from that—it's often filled with challenges, messiness, and constant difficulty.

Navigating Jealously and Insecurity
with my Associate Pastor

Sanetta is a pastor whom I greatly admire. She joined the Metro staff several years ago to oversee our community center and the Justice, Advocacy, and Compassion ministry in the church. Sanetta possesses immense gifts and brilliance. She earned her undergraduate degree from Columbia University and went on to pursue a JD at Harvard Law School, feeling called to be a lawyer after college. However, during her final year of law school, she felt God's calling to full-time ministry. Following her graduation from law school, she made the decision to pivot to seminary, where she earned her Master of Divinity at Duke Theological Seminary.

Not only is Sanetta exceptionally intelligent, but she is also a gifted communicator. She regularly delivers sermons at Metro, and her words never fail to inspire and bless those who listen.

There was a moment when Sanetta was invited to preach at Ebenezer Baptist Church in Englewood for their annual Martin Luther King service. The atmosphere was electric, with the venue packed to the brim—standing room only. Attendees from both Metro Community Church and Ebenezer Baptist Church filled the space, alongside the mayor, Englewood council members, and other county officials. Sanetta delivered a sermon that resonated deeply with the audience, eliciting applause and fervent "amens" in response to her powerful message.

After the service, two individuals from Metro approached me with unexpected remarks. The first said, "Peter, Sanetta preaches better than you." While this was not the feedback I had hoped for, I simply smiled and nodded in response. The second comment, however, caught me off guard: "Hey, Sanetta is so good that I think she is going to replace you one day at Metro." Shocked by the audacity of the statement, I couldn't help but wonder why someone would say such a thing to me. Did they not realize the potential impact of their words? Although I understand that individuals are entitled to their opinions, these remarks left me feeling unsettled and hurt. Despite striving for emotional health, I couldn't help but be affected by these comments.

Several months later, Sanetta began receiving invitations to speak at church planting conferences. Being respectful, she never accepted these invitations without seeking my approval first. When she informed me of these invitations, I couldn't help but feel a twinge of jealousy. Thoughts raced through my mind: "Why are they asking Sanetta to speak at these conferences? After all, I'm the one who planted the church!"

To compound matters, my friends who were church planters and denominational church planting directors would attend these conferences. Upon hearing Sanetta preach, they would enthusiastically message me, using fire emojis to convey their admiration. It felt as though they were igniting a flame within me, but it wasn't one of inspiration—it was one of insecurity. It seemed as though her presence reinforced the notion that I was somehow inadequate, that my own role in church planting was overshadowed. Unfortunately, this wasn't a one-time occurrence; it happened multiple times, each instance stoking the flames of jealousy within me.

The climax of my feelings occurred during a church pastors gathering in NYC. I got there early and was delighted to see New York bagels being offered to the participants. As I casually prepared a bagel, spreading cream cheese on it, a young pastor from Brooklyn approached me. "Are you Peter Ahn?" he asked. Finally, I thought, someone recognized me! "Yes, I am," I replied eagerly. Then, he dropped a bombshell: "My name is Tom, and I want you to know that I attended a church planting conference a few months ago. Sanetta preached, and she transformed my life. I've invited her to preach at my church in Brooklyn."

My heart sank, and I nearly lost my composure. I wanted to grab my bagel and smack Tom with it. Inside, I was seething. I wanted to retort, "Hey, Tom, why not listen to one of my sermons on www.emetro.org? Maybe you'll find it awesome too! Perhaps you'd consider inviting me to preach at your church instead of Sanetta!" But, of course, I remained composed. Through gritted teeth, I managed to respond, acknowledging Sanetta's greatness while inwardly feeling crushed.

I recognized that I wasn't in a good place emotionally. Each time Sanetta approached me about speaking engagements at churches or conferences, it felt as if a piece of me was slowly crumbling away. Bitterness toward Sanetta crept in, and I began to question her motives. The words of the person at the MLK service echoed in my mind: "Hey, Sanetta is so good that I think she is going to replace you one day at Metro." It became clear to me that I was not able to process my emotions adequately.

I am deeply thankful for my experience in the D.Min program at Alliance Theological Seminary. The inaugural class, led by Dr. Rob Reimer, delved into the insidious effects of shame on a leader's effectiveness. It was during these enlightening sessions that I began to recognize the significant role shame had played in my relationship with Sanetta.

Acknowledging my own shortcomings, I repented for my feelings toward Sanetta and sought forgiveness from God. With each prayerful plea, I felt a weight lift from my shoulders, preparing me to fully engage in the class. Yet, a quiet voice persisted, urging me to seek reconciliation with Sanetta. Despite my reservations, I couldn't ignore the prompting.

Summoning the last remnants of courage, I stepped into her office days later, quietly closing the door behind me. Vulnerably, I shared my struggles with Sanetta, seeking her forgiveness. Though surprised by what I shared, she graciously extended forgiveness and offered her prayers for me. In that moment, as she prayed, I experienced a profound revelation—God's divine calling on Sanetta's life. It became clear to me that the Church had marginalized the voices of women, particularly in the proclamation of God's Word. Through Sanetta, God intended to challenge this silence, inviting both women and men to learn from her voice. The realization left me overwhelmed with emotion.

Driving home that day, tears streaming down my face, I couldn't help but ponder the alternative. Without embracing emotional health, I might have fired Sanetta because she was a threat to my success. It was a sobering realization of the transformative power of emotional healing and forgiveness.

Pastors, let us remember that our calling from God is not rooted in success but in faithfulness. Failure to delve deep into the depths of our souls may lead us to minister solely from our strengths, driven by a desire for success. In this pursuit, we may even find ourselves feeling threatened by the presence of gifted and talented individuals whom God brings into our church staff.

Who are you hurting today? Is it yourself? Is it your church? Or is it your family? If we do not grow in emotional health, we will end up hurting the people we love the most.

A Weak Church and its leaders prioritize faithfulness over mere success. Let us, as pastors and church leaders, earnestly attend to our emotional health, recognizing its pivotal role in leading a weak church with God's strength and humility.

One often overlooked avenue for nurturing emotional health as adults is the pursuit of a soul mate. In the next chapter, we will explore this topic.

Notes

1. Jeff Hoglen, "Overcoming Fear of Failure: Plant a Thriving Church," *Church-planting.com*, May 8, 2023, accessed September 9, 2024, https://churchplanting .com/overcome-the-fear-of-failure-in-church-planting/#:~:text=Estimates%20vary %20between%2050%25%2D,first%20few%20months%20of%20operation.

2. Peter Scazzero, *Emotionally Healthy Spirituality* (Grand Rapids: Zondervan Reflective, 2006), 7.

3. Amy Volstad, "Emotionally Healthy Vs. Spiritually Healthy," *Christian Counselors Collaborative*, June 27, 2017, accessed January 21, 2023, https://www.cccpgh.org /emotionally-healthy-vs-spiritually-healthy/.

4. Ibid.

5. Dov Heller, "Eight Habits of Emotionally Healthy People," *AISH*, accessed January 21, 2023, https://aish.com/eight-habits-of-emotionally-healthy-people/.

6. 1 Corinthians 8:1.

7. Ibid., 15.

8. Michal Mitchell, "Eight Habits that Destroy Your Emotional Well Being," *Psy2Go*, September 4, 2020, accessed January 21, 2023, https://psych2go.net/8-habits -that-destroy-your-emotional-well-being/.

9. 2 Corinthians 12:9.

10. Hebrews 2:17.

11. Hebrews 4:15.

12. John Calvin, Commentary on the Gospel according to John, vol. 1 (Grand Rapids, 2003), 440.

13. Peter Scazzero, *Emotionally Healthy Leader* (Grand Rapids: Zondervan, 2015), 25.

14. Scazzero, *Emotionally Healthy Spirituality*, 179.

~

CHAPTER 4

Soul Mates

Becoming Fully Known

During my inaugural semester at Fuller Theological Seminary, I was incredibly excited about my upcoming classes. Jenny and I had journeyed cross-country from New Jersey to California, and the very air of Pasadena felt like a surreal fulfillment of our dreams. As I settled into one of my earliest courses, "Foundation of Ministry," taught by the esteemed Dr. Chap Clark, I found myself among roughly a hundred eager students awaiting his entrance into the auditorium. Dr. Clark's reputation as a dynamic communicator preceded him, sparking a high level of anticipation. We hungered for the profound insights and mic drop moments that awaited us from his lectures.

When Dr. Clark finally walked in, he was lugging this huge painting of Rembrandt's "Prodigal Son," blocking most of his body from view. He plunked it down on top of a black grand piano for everyone to see and then he shouted, "Why in the world do you want to be a pastor?! Don't you know it's like one of the worst jobs in America? It's the second worst, to be exact." I couldn't help but wonder what the first and third worst jobs were. With a grin, Dr. Clark said: "Third place goes to folks handling dynamite—not exactly the safest gig!" We all cracked up at the unexpected comparison. Dr. Clark had us hooked, waiting for the big reveal of America's most dreaded job.

With a serious tone, he said, "Being a logger is the toughest job in America. It's super dangerous—more folks get hurt falling from trees than in any other job!" I was totally shocked. Then he added, "And you know what? Pastoral work comes in second. No other profession destroys the family unit more than the office of clergy." His words hit me hard, wiping away any fancy ideas I had about being a pastor. "Here's something to chew on," he added, "pastors tend to live about ten years less than the average person.

Also, in your church, people might only show you love and acceptance based on what you can do for them, not who you are. And God forbid you start preaching bad sermons, they might not be as forgiving. And if you happen to treat yourself to a nice car, be prepared for some gossip to start spreading."

"Why do you want to be a pastor?!" Dr. Clark's question lingered in the air, making me almost blurt out my own doubts. Was moving to Pasadena for seminary a big mistake?

Then, Dr. Clark gestured toward Rembrandt's masterpiece, drawing our attention to it. "The reason you've said 'yes' to ministry boils down to one thing: You're God's beloved, and He is well pleased with you" he declared. But then, he threw us a curveball. "To really get that," he said, "you've got to open up about your deepest struggles with someone you trust—your soul mate." He emphasized how crucial it is to regularly confess our sins, saying that without that kind of closeness, our work in ministry wouldn't last long, and we'd start seeing pastoring as one of the toughest jobs around.

Soul Mate Defined

What defines a soul mate? A soul mate transcends the confines of marital or romantic relationships. Rather, a soul mate is someone of the same gender with whom you share a profound connection, a confidant to whom you reveal the darkest areas to your humanity. They are the ones who grant you the courage to embrace vulnerability and imperfection. Often, the pressure to present a facade of perfection and strength compels us into lives of secrecy, allowing our dark side to fester within us. Yet, in the presence of a soul mate, there lies a transformative power in embracing transparency, in being fully seen and known.

In essence, cultivating soul mate relationships echoes the essence of returning to Eden, to a state akin to that of Adam and Eve before the fall. It's an invitation to live authentically, without the burden of hidden truths, and to experience the profound freedom that comes with being fully understood and accepted.

In Genesis 2:25, it's written that "Adam and his wife were both naked, and they felt no shame." They were completely open and vulnerable with each other. No secrets, no hidden agendas—just pure, unfiltered connection. Back then, there was no need to hide any dark corners of their hearts because sin hadn't entered the picture yet. They were fully known and fully accepted. It wasn't just about physical nakedness; it was about the depth of their relationship, unencumbered by any barriers.

This is the kind of Eden we're called to live in—a place of deep connection and nakedness. Because of Jesus Christ's sacrifice on the cross and resurrection, he's paved the way for us to return to that Eden-like state. But to do so, we need to be willing to be vulnerable with a select few people in our lives—to let down our guard and be truly naked, emotionally and spiritually.

It's not a walk in the park, that's for sure. The urge to avoid real intimacy can be overwhelming—it's like a tidal wave crashing down on us, threatening to sweep us away. Our culture, and even the church, don't exactly cheer for this kind of deep connection. Instead, we're encouraged to hide our faults and weaknesses, to put on a facade of perfection and carry on like everything's fine. Small wonder why so many folks are wrestling with mental health issues these days.

Jesus is extending us an invitation back to Eden—a taste of heaven right here on earth. But we won't truly experience the sweetness of heaven unless we're willing to open up, invite someone in, and share the full spectrum of ourselves—the good, the bad, and the ugly.

There's a profound power waiting for us when we take this step. However, if we choose to stay closed off, our shame will grip us tightly, leading us down a path that Jesus never intended for us. Just like Adam and Eve, who, after their first misstep, suddenly felt exposed and hid themselves away. Their nakedness became a barrier, causing them to hide not just from each other, but from God too. "Then the eyes of both of them were opened, and they realized they were naked; so they sewed fig leaves together and made coverings for themselves. Then the man and his wife heard the sound of the LORD God as he was walking in the garden in the cool of the day, and they hid from the LORD God among the trees of the garden. But the LORD God called to the man, 'Where are you?' He answered, 'I heard you in the garden, and I was afraid because I was naked; so I hid.'"[1]

That's what sin does—it isolates us, driving us to conceal our true selves. If we don't open up and share our darkest struggles with someone, we'll inevitably follow suit, retreating into the shadows and distancing ourselves from both others and God.

Overcome Shame Not Weakness

In the summer of 2024, I led a Weak Church Conference for the Lahu Tribe in Thailand. The Lahu people are farmers, and many of their pastors are bi-vocational, balancing ministry with farming. With the help of an interpreter, I was deeply encouraged to see how much the pastors resonated with the weak church philosophy. It was a powerful reminder that recognizing our commonality through weakness and pain is one of the best ways to connect with people from diverse cultures, languages, and lifestyles.

While having lunch with the pastors, one of them asked, "How do I overcome my weakness? Please teach me how!" I told him that we should never try to overcome our weakness. Why would we want to eliminate something that is our superpower? If God perfects His strength in our weakness, then the goal is not to overcome it but to embrace it as much as possible. I explained that the desire to overcome weakness stems from the shame we feel from it. The true goal is not to overcome our weakness but to overcome our shame.

Shame destroys our capacity to see our weakness as a superpower. It whispers lies, convincing us that we must either overcome or hide our weaknesses. This pervasive shame is the greatest enemy to people wanting to embrace their weakness. It paralyzes us, creating a barrier that prevents us from acknowledging and accepting our imperfections. For pastors and church leaders, shame is particularly insidious. It can incapacitate them, hindering their ability to lead by example. When shame takes hold, it robs leaders of the courage to embrace and display their own weaknesses, thereby preventing them from fostering an environment where others can do the same. Instead of nurturing a culture of vulnerability and grace, shame perpetuates a façade of perfection, stifling genuine connection and growth within the community. The battle against shame is therefore crucial, not only for personal healing but also for empowering leaders to inspire and guide their congregations toward a more honest and liberated way of living.

Shame is a powerful and dangerous force that many people underestimate. Shame is an emotion that carries immense weight and consequences. It's not something to be brushed off lightly. When shame takes root, it has the power to wreak havoc in every corner of our lives. It drives us to conceal our true selves, trapping us in a cycle of secrecy and hiding.

In its grip, we're held captive, forced to live as a distorted version of who we truly are—a far cry from the freedom and wholeness that Jesus sacrificed himself for. That's the extent of shame's power.

The Power of SHAME

Shame is a universal emotion that impacts every human heart. Yet, for some, its grip tighter, its weight heavier. Robert Karen defines shame as: "The pathological belief that one is at the core a deformed being, fundamentally unlovable and unworthy of membership in the human community. It is the self-regarding the self with the withering and unforgiving eye of contempt."[2] Individuals who live in shame retreat to isolation, often creating a false self in order to protect their true selves from getting hurt. "When we are in the middle of a shame storm, it feels virtually impossible to turn again to see the face of someone, even someone we might otherwise feel safe with. It is as if our only refuge is in our isolation; the prospect of exposing what we feel activates our anticipation of further shame."[3] *Vulnerability stands as the sole antidote to shame.* According to Robert Karen and Curt Thompson, embracing vulnerability entails sharing one's deepest, darkest secrets with another soul. In this courageous act of disclosure, individuals not only open themselves to experiencing the profound grace and mercy of God but also liberate themselves from the suffocating grip of shame. "In some circumstances we anticipate this vulnerable exposure to be so great that it will be almost life threatening. But it is in the movement toward another, toward connection with someone who is safe, that we come to know life and freedom from this prison."[4] Yes, the prospect of such vulnerability can feel daunting, even life-threatening. But it's precisely in reaching out to another, in forging genuine connections with those who offer safety and understanding, that we discover true life and freedom.

One of the key purposes of a soul mate is to help us practice vulnerability, which will free us from the powerful grip of shame. By sharing the darkest areas of our humanity with our soul mate, we invite God's strength to dismantle the power of shame in our lives.

To cultivate a culture of vulnerability within a church, it must encourage its members to engage in soul mate relationships. This approach allows members to confront their deep-seated shame directly through honest confessions to their soul mate. In this courageous act of vulnerability, the chains of shame are shattered, leading to a newfound freedom from the prison that once confined them.

Leading by Example

The pastors and leaders of the church play a pivotal role in shaping the community's ethos and guiding its members by example. It is crucial that they embrace the value of nurturing deep, soulful connections within their own lives, exemplifying what it means to be in genuine communion with a soul mate. By doing so, they not only set a cultural tone within the congregation but also create a practical means for overcoming their own shame.

Leading by example, these spiritual guides illustrate the beauty and strength found in sharing life's journey with a kindred spirit. Their commitment to cultivating a soulful partnership serves as a beacon of inspiration, encouraging others within the church to seek and cherish meaningful connections of their own.

In essence, the pastors and leaders stand at the forefront, not only as spiritual mentors but also as living embodiments of the principles they espouse. Through their own experiences of companionship and mutual support, they instill within the community a deep-seated understanding of the transformative power inherent in soul mate relationships. Thus, they lead by example for the entire congregation to embrace a culture of vulnerability, empathy, and love.

A Closer Look at Shame from Shame Experts

Shame is not just another emotion; rather, it is a primary emotion that hijacks our ability to live healthy and connected lives. In *I Thought It Was Just Me*, Brené Brown writes that people's imperfections should never be seen as being inadequate or deterrents to being in healthy relationships. She argues that imperfections are what connects people to one another and to one's humanity. Being vulnerable about our imperfections with one another is a powerful reminder that everyone struggles and it's what actually brings people together in solidarity. However, when people choose to hide their imperfections, shame sets in and destroys one's ability to be in real healthy relationships. Brown defines shame as "the intensely painful feeling or experience of believing we are flawed and therefore unworthy of acceptance and belonging."[5] Brown contends that despite our society's relatively new openness to discussing other emotions like fear and anger, conversations surrounding shame remain taboo. Most people do not openly share their shame with others.[6] This is no different within the Church and the Christian community. While the Church must take some responsibility for failing to create safe spaces for individuals, oftentimes, it is also the feeling of shame that prevents people from being able to share openly and vulnerably. Shame tells us that we are unworthy of true belonging.

The greatest enemy of a weak church is the shame its people carry. A church cannot become a vulnerable community without helping and equipping its members to form soul mate relationships. If the key to overcoming shame is being vulnerable with someone, then the Church must recognize that a soul mate is not just an option for our spirituality—it is a dire necessity.

Dr. Curt Thompson, in *The Soul of Shame*, reveals shame's ubiquitous nature and neurobiological roots. He argues that shame affects every aspect of one's personal life and vocational endeavors. Shame destroys a Christian's identity in Christ, replacing it with a damaged version of themselves that results in unhealed pain and brokenness. Thompson writes, "shame most primitively and powerfully undermines the process of joyful attachment, integration and creativity."[7] When we live in shame, we live with an inherent fear of exposing our real selves. We separate from others due to the fear that if we get too close, others will discover who we really are. We create a different version of ourselves, sacrificing authenticity for acceptance.

Brené Brown goes deep into this topic of trying to fit in, *The Gift of Imperfection*. Too many people are exhausting their energy to try to fit in. How many times have people in the church focused their energy in trying to fit in with the Body of Christ? Brown argues that fitting in should never be the goal in the relationships that people pursue. "Fitting in and belonging are not the same thing, and, in fact, fitting in gets in the way of belonging. Fitting in is about assessing a situation and becoming who you need to be to be accepted. Belonging, on the other hand, doesn't require us to change who we are; it requires us to be who we are."[8] Brown believes that shame forces people to fit in out of fear that their imperfections might get exposed. She has empowered millions to bravely embrace vulnerability, inviting them to share their imperfections openly and authentically in order to find true belonging, rather than simply conforming to fit in.

Pastors and Church leaders will be profoundly blessed by teaching and supporting their members in forming soul mate relationships. This will empower individuals to move beyond merely trying to fit in and instead find a genuine sense of belonging within the church community. When this happens, shame no longer has the power to paralyze the congregation to become a Weak Church.

Sandra Wilson's *Into Abba's Arms* continues this discussion about shame and how it destroys one's ability to believe that he or she is lovable. Wilson argues that until people can learn to identify and overcome their shame, they will be unable to accept their true selves. If people cannot accept their true selves, then it will be impossible for them to show their true selves to others. Shame is the reason why this happens. She says, "shame is as if you are standing alone on one side of a broken bridge while everyone else in the world stares at you from the other side."[9]

Shame doesn't remind people that they are capable of making mistakes, it shouts that they are the mistake. Guilt can be forgiven, but shame forces one to cease to exist. Kevin Butcher writes that "shame is the satanic antithesis of God's love."[10] Shame is Satan's favorite weapon, and he loves to wield it and lead God's people to sin. "Shame is the primary tool that evil leverages, out of which emerges everything that we would call sin."[11]

The remedy for shame lies in vulnerability. It entails embracing complete transparency, but not with everyone—rather, with a trusted few in our lives whom we call "soul mates." These individuals journey with us through life, intimately acquainted with the darkest corners of our humanity. Soul mates don't just see the positive aspects of who we are; they also confront our deepest shadows. They're unafraid to speak truth with love, offering the feedback necessary for us to grow in greater self-awareness. It's in this sacred bond that people feel comfortable confessing their weakest and darkest aspects, with no secrets held back. Soul mates know us fully, and in return, we know them intimately as well.

Jesus Christ's sacrifice on the Cross wasn't merely to enable us to function—it was to grant humanity the power to conquer shame. "For the joy set before him he endured the cross, scorning its shame, and sat down at the right hand of the throne of God."[12] Kevin Butcher writes that in order to live a life of freedom our shame must be dealt with our willingness to be vulnerable. "Your shame cannot be privately wished away. It needs healing. Vulnerability met by the powerful, embodied love of Jesus Christ heals us and sets us free."[13]

Brené Brown acknowledges the challenging journey of embracing vulnerability as a means to overcome shame. She firmly asserts that there is no alternative path to defeating shame; one must be prepared to courageously share the darkest aspects of their humanity in order to break free from its grasp.

> When we can let go of what other people think and own our story, we gain access to our worthiness—the feeling that we are enough just as we are and that we are worthy of love and belonging. When we spend a lifetime trying to distance ourselves from the parts of our lives that don't fit with who we think we're supposed to be, we stand outside of our story and hustle for our worthiness by constantly performing, perfecting, pleasing and proving . . . love is the mirror image of shame. We desperately don't want to experience shame, and we're not willing to talk about it. Yet the only way to resolve shame is to talk about it.[14]

Sacrificing who one is for the sake of pleasing other people is not a worthy task. Jesus came and died for the real version of ourselves, not the fake version that we like to portray to others. When Christians, as followers of Jesus, choose not to be vulnerable in relationships, they will then be unable to love themselves fully. This inability, in turn, will render us incapable of loving our neighbor and God.

The only way Christians can love God and neighbor is by first loving themselves. This is in line with the Great Commandment, "Love the Lord your God with all your heart and with all your soul and with all your mind and with all your strength. The second is this: love your neighbor as your-self. There is no commandment greater than these."[15] If Christians choose not to engage in a consistent soul mate relationship, they very possibly will live inauthentic lives in which they are never fully known. They will be defenseless to the power of shame that may lead to other destructive men-tal issues. Brown gives a stern warning to her readers, "if you trade in your authenticity for safety, you may experience the following: anxiety, depres-sion, eating disorders, addiction, rage, blame, resentment, and inexplicable grief."[16]

In a Strong Church, the concept of soul mate relationships often takes a backseat. It's rarely discussed from the pulpit, and the practice of confessing to a soul mate is seldom modeled by leaders. Instead, when Christians gather for prayer, the focus tends to center on personal needs and desires. Operating within a framework that emphasizes strengths, congregants often struggle to open up about their weaknesses and sins, fearing the sting of shame.

In prayer groups, individuals frequently mask their true struggles behind a facade of spirituality, offering up superficial prayer requests that lack authen-ticity and depth. As a result, Monica Geyen argues, the church becomes a breeding ground for loneliness—a stark departure from its intended purpose as a community of believers. Indeed, the very essence of the Godhead, char-acterized by the unity of the Father, Son, and Holy Spirit, underscores the importance of community. "Many of our churches today have left behind that picture of the family of God, though. The contemporary Western church's 'absolutely low or nonexistent culture of family of God' has fostered an unparalleled depth of loneliness."[17]

Yet many contemporary Western churches have drifted from this ideal, failing to cultivate a genuine sense of familial connection among their mem-bers. Christians' desire to fit in rather than truly belong has led to feelings of loneliness within the church. Our shame fuels this loneliness, and despite numerous events and opportunities to connect, we may still feel isolated. This is because our shame often drives us to form superficial social relation-ships rather than deep connections where we truly feel like we belong.

In a Weak Church, the lead pastor and teaching team consistently empha-size the significance of soul mate relationships from the pulpit. Not content with mere words, they embody this concept in their own lives, serving as living examples of the profound transformation that occurs when individuals dare to be authentically vulnerable with one another.

Their actions inspire the congregation to follow suit, fostering a culture where members freely confess their shortcomings and share their struggles. In this environment of radical transparency, individuals confront their brokenness head-on, yet simultaneously experience the powerful grace of God at work in their lives.

Here, true holiness isn't measured by outward deeds, but rather by the depth of one's vulnerability. By opening up to their soul mates and confessing their sins and receiving feedback, individuals embrace their vulnerability and brokenness, liberating themselves from the grip of shame.

This vulnerability uniquely equips Christians to walk alongside others who, like themselves, are bruised and vulnerable. As Butcher aptly puts it, "the intimate connection with other brothers and sisters in the body of Christ isn't arbitrary or optional but like breathing—absolutely necessary for life in our relationship with Jesus."[18]

Engaging in soul mate relationships allows Christians to regularly shed the façade of who they think they should be, embracing their authentic selves with all their imperfections. Soul mates provide the courage to embrace their flaws and vulnerabilities, fostering an environment where imperfection is not only accepted but celebrated.

When we openly share our dark side with our soul mate, they do more than just listen—they offer valuable feedback. Just as iron sharpens iron, our soul mates play a crucial role in our spiritual growth—they encourage, question, challenge, and even rebuke us, guiding us to live as disciples of Jesus Christ. They do this with a deep sense of love and care for our well-being.

As a spiritual mentor once told me, "While Jesus might let us get away with sins (meaning Jesus will forgive us of any sin), your soul mate should never turn a blind eye. They should push you to examine your actions more deeply, preventing you from falling into repeated patterns of sin."

Vulnerability isn't a quality one either possesses or lacks; rather, it's a skill that requires deliberate practice. The pathway to overcoming shame lies in opening up completely to someone, relinquishing the burden of secrets and allowing oneself to be fully known.

In this journey toward vulnerability, Christians discover that their worth isn't earned through striving, but rather bestowed upon them as beloved children of the King of Kings. Freed from the need to hustle for their value, they rest secure in the knowledge of their royal identity.

The Nuts and Bolts of Living in Soul Mate Relationships

How to Find a Soul Mate

Finding a soul mate can often feel like a daunting journey, but it doesn't have to be overwhelming. The prospect of confessing our sins to someone is challenging enough, and the idea of finding a soul mate can seem like an insurmountable task. Throughout my years of pastoring at Metro Community Church, I have encountered countless individuals eager to cultivate soul mate relationships yet struggling to find the right connection.

To address this need, we offer a Soul Mate Workshop designed to equip participants with practical tools for fostering intimate relationships rooted in vulnerability and trust. This workshop takes individuals step by step through the process of cultivating deep, meaningful connections, offering valuable insights and actionable strategies for building a soul mate relationship. The workshop generally covers the following steps.

1. Pray

     Prayer stands as the cornerstone in the search for a soul mate. It's through prayer that we align our desires with God's plan for community, and when we earnestly seek His guidance, He won't withhold this blessing from us. Dedicate time to praying to our heavenly Father to lead you to your soul mate.

     However, prayer alone isn't enough. It's essential to take proactive steps in your search. Remain intentional and purposeful as you actively seek out potential connections. While you pray, keep a keen eye on the people who have crossed your path, both in the past and in your present.

2. Seek Out a Same Sex Christian Soul Mate[19]

     It's paramount that your soul mate is a Christian. This is because of Jesus' promise: "For where two or three gather in my name, there am I with them."[20] Therefore, it's essential that your soul mate in confession is a fellow believer. There's no room for compromise here; Jesus assures his presence when believers gather in his name.

     Additionally, your soul mate must be of the same sex. Opening up completely to someone of the opposite sex can be challenging, as men and women often face gender-specific struggles. It's not feasible for a spouse to fulfill this role; they may struggle to fully understand and accept certain sins, such as attraction to others, or issues within the marriage. Therefore, it's crucial that your soul mate is both a Christian and of the same sex.

3. Look for High Character and Integrity

     The best soul mates are individuals of impeccable character and unwavering integrity. Seek out those in your life who embody these traits. While shared interests and spiritual maturity can be beneficial, they pale in comparison to the significance of character and integrity. For instance, one of my soul mates is a police officer. Although he may not share all of my interests or is in full-time ministry, his remarkable character and integrity make him a perfect soul mate. When searching for a soul mate, prioritize finding someone of exemplary character and integrity above all else.

4. Making the Ask

Once you've identified a potential candidate, it's time to make the ask. Here are the criteria and expectations for a soul mate:

- **Confidentiality:** Establish the highest level of confidentiality. What is shared between soul mates remains between them and is never disclosed to anyone else.
- **Lifelong Friendship:** Understand that this friendship is for life. The deep confessions and shared experiences between soul mates are sacred and meant to be preserved for a lifetime.
- **Regular Meetings:** Commit to meeting at least twice a month to mutually confess sins and share life updates. This can be done in person, over the phone, or via video conferencing. Both parties must be intentional about maintaining this frequency to prevent forgetting sins or minimizing their significance.
- **Speaking Truth in Love:** Encourage each other to speak truth into one another's lives. Grant your soul mate permission to provide feedback and ask questions on the sins you're struggling with. No topics should be off-limits, and both parties should actively seek and welcome constructive feedback. Without this honest dialogue, the soul mate relationship becomes ineffective.
- **Forgiveness:** After confessing sins, the soul mate should affirm forgiveness by saying, "because you have confessed your sins, your sins are forgiven." Hearing these words reassures that sins are forgiven. "If you forgive anyone's sins, their sins are forgiven; if you do not forgive them, they are not forgiven."[21] Remember, Jesus is present when believers gather, and they can extend forgiveness to one another.
- **Life Confession:** Share the greatest sins you've committed in your life that you've kept hidden. This is non-negotiable. A life confession can be transformative.
- **Annual Vacation:** Take intentional time away with your soul mate at least once a year. While the relationship is serious, it's also important to have fun and nurture the bond away from the stresses of work and family.

How Important Is Our Soul Mate?

Our soul mates hold a profound significance in our lives. They're not merely friends; they're the individuals with whom we share our deepest selves. As such, they play a vital role in our overall well-being. Whether you're married or single, here's the order of importance:

Married
1. God
2. Spouse
3. Kids/Soul Mate
4. Family
5. Friends

My soul mates hold a significance in my life that surpass the importance of my parents and siblings due to the unique intimacy shared between us. They are just as important as my children.

Single
1. God
2. Soul Mate
3. Family
4. Friends
5. Dating Relationship

Only God surpasses the importance of a soul mate for a single person.

Whether married or single, prioritizing this relationship offers the opportunity to dwell in Eden regularly. Rather than merely visiting Eden, you become a permanent resident on earth.

Returning to Eden entails living life akin to Adam and Eve before their first sin—an idea encapsulated in "realized eschatology," where we experience a glimpse of heaven on earth. This return enables us to rediscover existence before sin tainted the world, epitomized by Adam and Eve's fearlessness while naked.

Embracing our vulnerabilities and being open with our soul mates is a return back to Eden—becoming "naked and not afraid." Shame has lost its sting and no longer holds power over our lives. While we may still encounter shame occasionally, it will no longer have the strength to control us. This aspect of Christianity is profound; we don't have to wait until death to experience heaven. Reviving this understanding within the church could spark a profound revival. The world yearns for the fearlessness of Eden, but our shame inhibits us from it.

Soul mates provide a pathway for Christians to return to Eden—to be "naked and not afraid." It's time to embrace this journey back to Eden.

I Almost Committed Adultery

In 2015, my world was shaken when my father passed away unexpectedly. Despite his eight-year stay in a nursing home, his death blindsided me, leaving me unprepared to face the loss. At the same time, Metro Community Church encountered a financial crisis due to the departure of key leaders and members. They disagreed with our outspoken stance on racial injustice—a gospel-driven pursuit that I preached passionately on Sundays. As people left in protest, our church faced a dire situation, with staff layoffs looming. I felt like a failure.

Amid this darkness, I grappled with the sin of lust and adultery in ways I'd never experienced during my marriage to Jenny. The allure of another woman seemed intoxicating amid the bitterness of my circumstances. I even considered creating a profile on a dating app or hiring a prostitute, especially while traveling.

I owe my resilience to my soul mate, a police officer, who possesses a natural inclination to probe deep into my struggles whenever I confess to him. During one such conversation about my battle with adultery, his words pierced through my soul: "Peter, you're going to lose everything. I'm not just talking about the church—I mean your wife and kids. STOP entertaining these ideas!" It felt as if Jesus Himself were speaking directly to me.

Though I wish I could say I immediately overcame my struggle with adultery, it persisted for over two years. Throughout this time, my soul mate remained steadfast in holding me accountable, continuously speaking words of truth into my soul. He frequently reminded me that I was not alone in my struggle. He would say, "Peter, if you go down, I go down with you. I'm not going to let you fight this battle alone. I've got your back." These words were some of the most life-giving I had ever heard from another person. Knowing that someone was there to support me, helping me fight against my sinful nature during this dark period of my life, was incredibly empowering.

A soul mate embodies God's presence in our lives, walking alongside us in the flesh. For a church to become weak, it must foster and guide its community toward such intimate connections. This endeavor begins with the lead pastor, pastoral staff, and extends to the elder and deacon board, all living within this intimate community. Jesus desires to manifest His presence in our lives and churches incarnationally.

The alternative is that not only will your church fail to become weak, but more importantly, you will live without fully embracing the truth that you are God's beloved child, in whom He delights.

Jesus longs to have a tangible presence in our lives and within our churches. Will you begin to pray earnestly for God's blessing to bring a soul mate into your life? And will you take deliberate steps, as outlined in this chapter, to cultivate this transformative relationship? The choice is ultimately between living in shame or dancing in the garden of Eden. The decision rests with you.

Notes

1. Genesis 3:7–10.

2. Robert Karen, "Shame," *The Atlantic Monthly*, February 2009, accessed May 4, 2021, http://www.empoweringpeople.net/shame/shame.pdf.

3. Curt Thompson, *The Soul of Shame* (Downers Grove: Intervarsity Press, 2015), 34.

4. Ibid., 35.

5. Brene Brown, *I Thought It Was Just Me* (New York: Penguin Random House, 2007), 5.

6. Ibid., 3.

7. Thompson, *The Soul of Shame*, 62.

8. Brene Brown, *The Gifts of Imperfection* (Minnesota: Hazelden Publishing, 2010), 25.

9. Sandra D. Wilson, *Released From Shame: Moving Beyond the Pain of the Past* (Downers Grove, IL: Intervarsity Press, 2002), 23.

10. Kevin Butcher, *Free* (Grand Rapids: NAV Press, 2021), 146.

11. Thompson, *The Soul of Shame*, 146.

12. Hebrews 12:2.

13. Butcher, *Free*, 156.

14. Brown, *The Gifts of Imperfection*, 23.

15. Mark 12:30–31.

16. Brown, *The Gifts of Imperfection*, 53.

17. Monica Geyen, "Is The Church Breeding Loneliness?" *Desiring God*, April 17, 2019, accessed January 21, 2023, https://www.desiringgod.org/articles/is-the-church-breeding-loneliness.

18. Butcher, *Free*, 127.

19. The distinction between "sex" and "gender" is widely examined in social literature. If you're interested in this topic, consider exploring further readings on the subject.

20. Matthew 18:20.

21. John 20:23.

CHAPTER 5

Incarnational Preaching

How many sermons have you listened to? I've heard thousands over the years. But how many of those sermons have made a transformative impact on your life? Sadly, probably not many. Why? The common issue with many sermons is an overemphasis on content. While content is important, the emphasis of a sermon should be more on cultivating culture.

As pastors, we must prioritize writing sermons that build the culture of the church rather than focus exclusively on content. While content is important, the key is how our sermons contribute to the kind of culture we want our church to embody. Preaching should aim to shape and nurture the church's culture first, and then focus on content. Missing this emphasis is missing the essence of incarnational preaching.

Seminaries often emphasize teaching students how to exegete the text, which is undoubtedly important. However, this heavy focus on content might be why there is so little life change in our congregations. The reality is that most people in our churches won't remember much of the content we preach. Personally, I don't mind if people forget the specifics of my sermon. While it would be nice if they remembered, what truly matters to me is how my sermon encourages people to become more vulnerable within our church community.

Building a culture of openness and weakness must start with the pastor, who should lead by sharing their own struggles in life on the pulpit. When a pastor shares vulnerably in their sermon, it allows the congregation to have an incarnational encounter with Jesus. If Jesus' strength is perfected in our weakness, then a pastor's transparency in preaching creates an opportunity for a tangible, concrete encounter with Jesus himself. This is incarnational preaching.

Incarnation literally means "in the flesh." Pastors should aim for their sermons to inspire congregants to embody the church's ministry culture. The true impact of a sermon is not measured by how well people remember the content, but by how it motivates them to live into the church's culture. The best sermons prioritize preaching culture over content.

Therefore, for a church to embrace and embody a ministry philosophy of weakness, it is critical for pastors to preach with transparency. This includes sharing their own struggles and how they have wrestled with their sinful nature, the enemy, and God. If preachers are not willing to do this, the church will fail to truly embody a posture of weakness.

Can a Pastor Share Too Much from the Pulpit?

What level of transparency should pastors aim for in their sermons? Go as far as you can, as long as there is a redemptive aspect to your story. While sharing your story, ensure that it includes how God is teaching and ministering to you. It can't be all darkness; there must be a redemptive quality.

Please remember that your story must not be arbitrary; it should connect with the text or sermon point you are preaching about. Your story shouldn't come out of nowhere. There must be a clear purpose for sharing your story in your sermon. Ensure that your story finds synergy with the text or sermon point you are discussing. This connection will bring your sermon to life, creating a moment where people can experience Jesus Christ "in the flesh." When your personal story aligns with the message, it becomes a powerful tool that not only illustrates the sermon's point but also allows the congregation to encounter God's work in a tangible and relatable way. Such moments can deeply resonate with listeners, fostering a stronger, more personal connection to the message and to Christ.

Establish an Emotional Connection
First in Your Sermons

The average attention span of an adult is eight seconds.[1] A sermon based on its good exegesis alone is not going to connect with today's people. The exegesis can be great, but in order to effectively preach to a congregation, the pastor/preacher must be able to emotionally connect with them. A strong exegetical sermon is necessary, but without the preacher's willingness to bring his or her life story into it, the sermon will often fall on deaf ears. A preacher must know that connecting with the congregation on an emotional level is going to be paramount. Bert Decker, a communication's guru and professor proclaims the importance of vulnerability when we give our messages. He writes that "by being vulnerable and open about our struggles, we make an emotional connection with our audience. This creates trust and believability . . . you've got to be trusted to be believed."[2]

There has been extensive study on the brain that supports this claim according to Decker. He states that communication is not a process of disseminating information, but emotionally connecting with your listeners.[3] The reason for this is because effective communication must initially penetrate the First Brain. The First Brain is "the nonreasoning, nonrational part of our brain." To put it simply, "it is the seat of human emotions, composed of the brain stem and the limbic system."[4] The First Brain is the gatekeeper for the New Brain. The New Brain is "the seat of conscious thought, memory, language, creativity, and decision making."[5] When people communicate through the spoken word, they have a tendency to always focus their message on the New Brain and completely overlook the First Brain. Decker argues that, for communicators to effectively impact their listeners, the role of the First Brain must be considered. He writes that "to reach the New Brain, our message must first pass through the First Brian, the emotional part of the brain. If we leave the First Brain out of the equation, our message will be distorted or diminished—or it may not get through at all."[6] It is the listener's First Brain that decides whether or not to trust and believe the speaker at all. "It's the First Brain that decides whether a person represents comfort and nurture—or anxiety and menace."[7] For Decker, real-life experiences are the most memorable because they have the deepest emotional impact.

In a Strong Church, pastors often preach sermons on Sundays from a place of strength in which they flex their theological muscles (sermons are solely content driven) or highlight their spiritual victories, rather than openly share their brokenness and sinfulness with their congregations. People listening to the sermons are not emotionally connected with the pastor. They often feel preached down to or believe that their pastors are Christian Super Stars whose lives have no relevance to their own. Decker calls these pastors *old communicators,* "an old communicator uses the spoken word to dispense information . . . Old communicators fail. You dare not make the mistake of thinking that communication is nothing but dumping information on another person."[8]

In a Weak Church, pastors bring authenticity to the next level by sharing the vulnerable and broken aspects of their humanity on Sundays. Redemption loses its value if we do not know what it is we have been redeemed from. When pastors share the dark and broken parts of their soul, God's redemption message is powerfully preached through their lives. This level of vulnerability creates an emotional connection that deepens trust between the preacher and the congregation. By doing this, the pastor sets the tone for transparency in the Church and cultivates a culture of weakness in the congregation. If the pastor does not embrace this philosophy, church members will not feel emboldened or convicted to share their own weaknesses with others.

Incarnational preaching is essential for fostering a weak church. For a pastor to preach in this manner, they must prioritize their emotional health and regularly confess their sins to a soul mate. Without this foundation, shame can inhibit a pastor, leading them out of fear to focus solely on the content of a sermon.

When a pastor is emotionally healthy and openly shares their struggles and darkest moments with a soul mate, they are empowered to preach more transparently. This vulnerability allows the congregation to emotionally connect with the pastor, providing hope and fostering a culture of openness within the church. Such authenticity can profoundly impact the church community, creating a space where people feel safe to embrace their own weaknesses and find strength in their shared experiences.

Being vulnerable on the pulpit is transformative. It allows pastors and leaders to connect on a deeper, more human level with their church members, demonstrating that it is okay to have struggles and imperfections. By openly discussing their own challenges, leaders set an example of authenticity and vulnerability, which can inspire the entire congregation to do the same. This creates a community where people feel safe to share their own weaknesses, fostering a culture of mutual support and understanding. Ultimately, it is this honest, shame-free environment that allows for genuine spiritual growth and connection.

This is why incarnational preaching is critical in a church's transition to becoming "weak." The only way to effectively become a weak church is when the pastor is willing to stand in front of the congregation and preach vulnerably; there is no other way. Every church in the world has one thing in common: a pastor will preach the sermon to their parishioners on Sunday. Steven Lawson in his article, *Why Is Preaching Important for Healthy Churches*,[9] contends that if a church removes or tries to minimize the preaching from its Sunday service, it is removing God's primary way for grace to be received. Lawson, a preaching professor, believes that the preaching of the sermon is indispensable to the church, and the more churches try to minimize the sermon, the less healthy they become. Jesus, himself, was a preacher. The Twelve Apostles were avid preachers. In the book of Acts, "one out of every five verses are a sermon or is a powerful witness, a verbal witness being given by the Apostle Paul. The book of Acts is a book of preaching."[10] The Apostle Paul in 2 Timothy 4:2 encourages church leaders to "Preach the word; be prepared in season and out of season; correct, rebuke and encourage—with great patience and careful instruction." Preaching originated in the very first church in Acts, and 2,000 years later, preaching is still the most essential component of a Sunday service for any church.

If all of this is true, then there is no better way to effectively establish the theological and cultural foundation of weakness in a church than through preaching. The focus of every sermon must be on building culture first, before addressing its content. Each Sunday, the pastor has the opportunity to teach the church the theological primacy of being weak and vulnerable through the litany of texts that are available through the Old and New Testament. But even more crucial than the text is the pastor becoming vulnerable through his or her own personal stories of weakness and brokenness.

Peter Scazzero, in his book *Emotionally Healthy Discipleship*, speaks of his own radical transformation toward becoming a weak and vulnerable senior pastor. Prior to 1996, Scazzero led out of strength via his successes. Strength-based leadership is a proud and defensive style of leadership. Due to the lack of emotional health, Scazzero's sermons were strength/success-based. His strength-based preaching played a significant role in his ideology of what a pastor/leader should portray to their congregation. As a result, Scazzero did everything he possibly could to avoid failure. Even though he failed consistently, he was too proud or defensive to admit it. Scazzero developed a chart in table 5.1 to compare the weak and vulnerable leadership modeled by Jesus in Gethsemane against the proud and defensive leadership that most leaders model today.

When Scazzero began taking steps to become emotionally healthy, his preaching was transformed radically. He writes about his experience in 1996: "I made the radical shift to preach out of my failures, weaknesses, and struggles, not my successes. Initially, this level of vulnerability was very uncomfortable and frightening. I began to wrestle with texts and my own difficulties in obeying them before I applied them to others. . . . I finally realized the most powerful part of the message was the power of Jesus coming through my own struggles to apply the text."[11] Scazzero believes that incarnational preaching allows the pastor and his or her congregation to be on "equal footing, wrestling to obey God's Word in our lives . . . creating a healthy discipleship culture flows out of who we are as leaders, which means the stakes are especially high in those moments when our weaknesses and flaws are exposed. And these moments come to all of us."[12]

Table 5.1   Weak and Vulnerable Leadership versus Proud and Defensive Leadership

Weak and Vulnerable	*Proud and Defensive*
I allow myself to be sorrowful and troubled in front of others.	I cover over my feelings of sorrow and confusion in front of my team.
I admit to my team when I am feeling overwhelmed.	I refuse to fall apart, always modeling strong faith and vision, especially in front of my team.
I easily ask for help and prayers of others.	I rarely appear needy in front of others. While I will be there for others, I don't look for others to be there for me.
I pray in utter dependence to surrender my will to God's will.	I pray how to strategically turn a bad situation around and expand the ministry.
I have no problem falling face down on the ground in front of others when I struggle to submit myself to the unfathomable will of the Father.	I try to stand tall, being decisive and unwavering in crisis, so others can lean on me for faith and strength.

Peter Scazzero, *Emotionally Healthy Discipleship* (Grand Rapids: Zondervan, 2021), 193.

Ryan Huguley, a pastor and writer for Christianity.com, stresses the importance of pastors leading and preaching out of places of vulnerability. He contends that when pastors preach and lead vulnerably, they do not bring attention to themselves, but to Jesus Christ. Huguley believes many pastors today struggle because of how people portray pastors—as the "ever-stable, always-faithful, never-failing rock." This causes some pastors to suffer in silence, struggle in secret, and suffocate in isolation. This sad tendency is destructive for the church, but deadly for the pastor.

> We live in a culture hungry for heroes. People are desperate to be delivered from whatever it is that ails them. In the church, this means the preacher/pastor is often held up as the hero everyone leans on, runs to, and trusts in to save them. The problem is, pastors are helpless sinners, not heroes. Sadly, some perpetuate this problem by celebrating their strengths, only discussing their sin in the past tense, and never opening up about their weaknesses. Conversely, when we as pastors lead from our vulnerability, it makes us human and points the people we shepherd to Jesus, the only true Hero we all need.[13]

I often wonder how many pastors would still be in ministry today if they felt empowered to share openly with their congregation. Too many have left because of the pressure to appear perfect or invulnerable. Pastors are not meant to be Jesus himself; rather, their calling is to point others to Him.

The most effective way to do this is through incarnational preaching—by openly sharing our own weaknesses with our congregation.

Incarnational preaching will allow the pastor to emotionally connect with the congregation and build trust. Once trust is established, the exegesis of the text will transform the person's life. The beautiful by-product of this is that the culture of weakness is extending from the pastor to the entire church. The congregation will feel emboldened to be vulnerable in their own Christian circles. The pastor empowers the congregation to be vulnerable by modeling this on the pulpit. Through this newly found vulnerability, the congregation members will experience a new kind of Christianity that will allow them to be comfortable in their own skin. No longer will they feel the need to hide or pretend to be someone they are not, but instead, they will embrace their true selves as they encounter the prefect strength of God.

Henri Nouwen calls every pastor around the world to lead out of a place of vulnerability. Pastors are called to lead in this way, not to claim a defeatist mentality, but so that they can learn to depend upon the guidance of Jesus Christ. Nouwen believes that when Christian leaders do not lead out of vulnerability, they run the risk of falling into the trap of wealth and success, which prevents leaders from discerning the ways of Jesus. Nouwen believes that the only way that pastors and Christian leaders can protect themselves from plunging into this kind of destructive ambition is to lead through vulnerability. He writes, "the Christian leader of the future is called . . . to stand in this world with nothing to offer but his or her own vulnerable self."[14]

Rick Warren warns pastors of what will happen should they choose not to lead out of vulnerability. Three things that happen to non-vulnerable pastors are:

1. Our weaknesses get worse, feeding off of the shame and secrecy.
2. We become dishonest and hypocritical.
3. The truth inevitably comes out and people are disillusioned as a result.[15]

Warren says that when pastors choose to be vulnerable, they will be able to gain the trust of their parishioners and staff. "We only follow leaders we trust. The first requirement for effective leadership is credibility, and the more *honest* you are, the more *credible* you become. Real leaders lead by example. They go first. If your desire is that the church, group, or organization you're leading be a place where people are open, you must be the first to open up.

You must decide whether you want to **impress** people (which you can do from a distance) or **influence** people (which you can only do up close)."[16]

Scott entered our church completely drained of life. He had declared bankruptcy on his company, watched his former church implode due to bad leadership, and ended a relationship with someone he thought he would marry. The severe loss and trauma he had sustained led Scott to have thoughts of ending his life.

Someone had told Scott about Metro Community Church. Despite his vow to never set foot in a church again, something prompted him to give Metro a try. That Sunday, I shared a deeply personal story about my abusive father and how I once contemplated taking his life because of the trauma he inflicted on our family. Scott couldn't believe what he was hearing. In all his years of attending church, he had never heard a pastor speak with such vulnerability. Though he didn't know me personally, Scott confessed, "I felt like I could trust Peter with my life." He recommitted his life to the Lord that day. This happened in 2008, and today, Scott is a missionary in Southeast Asia, impacting the lives of women and men with the ministry philosophy of weakness. His journey from despair to purpose stands as a testament to the transformative power of incarnational preaching.

What Scott encountered that Sunday was nothing short of a divine revelation through Jesus Christ. As I laid bare my weaknesses, pains, and struggles, the strength of God was made perfect in my story. When these words reached Scott's ears, it wasn't merely human testimony he was hearing—it was the Holy Spirit at work, transforming his life completely. In that moment, he experienced a profound and undeniable connection with God's grace and mercy. The impact was so powerful that Scott knew he would never be the same again. His heart was revived, his faith renewed, and his path redirected toward a purpose he could have never imagined during his darkest days. This encounter marked the beginning of a new chapter in Scott's life, one filled with hope, healing, and a commitment to sharing the transformative love of Christ with others through his weakness.

How to Craft an Incarnational Sermon

Preaching is an art form. The more you work at it and practice, the better you will become. I encourage preachers to read widely, attend preaching workshops, and study the preachers they admire. If you are not willing to put in the effort to become an effective preacher, you probably won't achieve that goal. Unfortunately, I encounter too many pastors who lack the desire to grow and improve as communicators. No matter how skilled you are, there is always room for growth.

One common mistake I see among preachers is turning to commentaries too early in the sermon preparation process. It's critical for pastors to wrestle with the text themselves and allow the Holy Spirit to speak to them first. These are the sermons that resonate most powerfully. When God speaks to you about a text, you preach with greater authority and anointing. While I understand the challenges of preparing weekly sermons, skipping this step and rushing to a commentary can lead to superficial sermons. Personally, I read the text repeatedly until the Holy Spirit speaks to me—sometimes over twenty times. Spending ample time on the text is essential.

Another common mistake I find among preachers is creating a sermon outline before thoroughly examining the text. This approach prevents the text from speaking to them organically. Instead, they develop an outline first and then search for passages to support it. This is not an effective way to preach. It's crucial to spend time with the biblical text. Although it may take longer, I guarantee that when the Holy Spirit speaks to you, your sermon will be far more impactful. Allow the text to shape your message, rather than fitting the text into a predetermined outline.

I'm also not a fan of relying heavily on sermon series. While they can be beneficial occasionally, there's no substitute for preaching directly through books of the Bible. In the past, church growth experts have suggested tailoring sermons to address people's felt needs, a model many mega-churches have adopted. These churches often use sermon series to attract the unchurched by focusing on relevant, felt needs. While this approach can effectively bring people into the church, I'm not convinced it has the same transformative power as sermons grounded in scripture.

The word of God never returns void. I encourage pastors to center their sermon series on books of the Bible rather than themes designed primarily to attract attendees. True church growth occurs when people encounter God's power through the authentic and vulnerable preaching of His Word. When a preacher's weaknesses are laid bare, God's strength is revealed, leading to profound transformation in the lives of the congregation.

Nuts and Bolts of Sermon Prep

1. Immerse Yourself in the Text

    Read the text you plan to preach on thoroughly. Remember, repetition is beneficial. Be patient and continue reading until the Holy Spirit speaks to you. Keep reading the text until you identify one central question you want to answer in your sermon. Focus on addressing that single question.

2. Crafting Focused Sermon Points

Develop two to three sermon points that directly answer your main question. Ensure these points are rooted in the text you are focusing on. Avoid relying on other texts to validate your points. Using additional scripture to reinforce the points already affirmed by the primary text is beneficial.

3. Deepen Your Understanding with Commentaries

Read commentaries to gain a deeper exegetical understanding of your text. If the commentaries contradict your sermon points, revise your points accordingly. This is uncommon, but it's essential to avoid preaching a false interpretation of the text. Use commentaries to validate your sermon points and enrich your exegetical comprehension of the text.

4. Personal Stories: Bridging the Gap

In each sermon point, incorporate a personal story. Sharing your own experiences will enable your congregation to connect with you on an emotional level. Personal stories bring your sermon to life, making it relatable and impactful. When you share your own struggles, triumphs, or insights, you create a bridge between the biblical text and the lived experiences of your audience. This emotional connection not only makes your message more memorable but also helps your listeners see the practical application of scripture in everyday life. Remember, vulnerability fosters trust and opens hearts, allowing your congregation to experience the transformative power of God's Word more deeply.

5. Crafting an Engaging Introduction

When crafting your introduction, envision a non-believer in your congregation asking, "So what? Why should I listen to your sermon?" If you can't answer that in your introduction, unchurched individuals may lose interest. Always prepare with the assumption that unchurched people are present and listening to your sermon. Don't forget to memorize your introduction.

6. Conclusion: The Heart of Your Sermon

Your conclusion is the pinnacle of your sermon, where hearts are moved and lives are touched. It's crucial to weave in a personal, vulnerable story that resonates deeply with your audience. Allow yourself to be open and transparent, sharing a moment of vulnerability that carries a redemptive message. Take your listeners on a journey to your own Gethsemane, where you faced your darkest moments. It's in this raw honesty that the power of redemption shines brightest. By sharing your struggles authentically, you create a connection that allows the redemptive part of your story to truly resonate.

7. Practice Makes Perfect

Dedicate time to practice your sermon repeatedly, aiming for 10–15 practice sessions. It may seem like a lot of effort, but internalizing your sermon is crucial. Without this internalization, you risk being tied to your notes, hindering your ability to connect with your congregation.

When you share personal stories, ensure they are memorized. This allows you to speak from the heart, maintain eye contact, and truly engage with your listeners.

8. The Importance of Feedback!

Before delivering your sermon to the congregation, preach it to your staff or, if you're a solo pastor, to your spouse. Seek honest feedback—this is crucial! Many pastors avoid this step due to insecurities, but overcoming this barrier is essential.

Professional speakers never debut their speech at the main event; they seek feedback and make revisions. At Metro, our preachers present their sermons to the pastoral staff on Thursday afternoons, receiving valuable feedback from colleagues with seminary degrees.

This should be a no brainer, yet so many pastors shy away from this. Please receive feedback on your sermon before preaching it to your congregation. This step is indispensable for delivering a powerful and effective message.

Final Charge

Pastors, what is holding you back from taking this leap? I understand the hesitation. No one likes to bare their soul publicly. Many times, I have felt exposed and vulnerable after sharing deeply with the congregation. It often felt as if I had stepped onto the stage physically naked. In the early days of Metro, I would go home and crawl into bed, feeling a profound sadness. I wish I could tell you that incarnational preaching will always leave you with warm, fuzzy feelings, but that is simply not the case. This is a sacrifice that clergy must be willing to make. I believe this is part of the cross Jesus has called pastors to bear.

Two decades later, it still isn't easy, but I have witnessed countless times how God uses my preaching to transform lives in ways that are profound and lasting. Pastors, this sacrifice is well worth it. In the end, a church cannot become truly weak if the preacher is not willing to be vulnerable in their sermons. Embrace the challenge, for it is through our weaknesses that God's strength is perfected and lives are transformed.

Notes

1. Bert Decker, *You've Got to Be Believed to be Heard* (New York: St. Martin's Press, 2008), 227.

2. Ibid., 99.

3. Ibid., 6.

4. Ibid., 71.

5. Ibid., 72.

6. Ibid., 73.

7. Ibid., 73.

8. Ibid., 31.

9. Steven J. Lawson, "Why Is Preaching Important For Healthy Churches," *Table Talk*, October 4, 2021, accessed November 5, 2021, https://tabletalkmagazine.com/posts/why-is-the-preaching-of-gods-word-vital-for-the-health-of-the-local-church/.

10. Ibid.

11. Scazzero, *Emotionally Healthy Discipleship*, 200–201.

12. Ibid., 201.

13. Ryan Huguley, "3 Reasons Pastors Need to Be Vulnerable," *Christianity.com*, August 3, 2014, accessed December 13, 2021, https://www.christianity.com/church/pastors/3-reasons-pastors-need-to-be-vulnerable-and-3-cautions.html.

14. Henri Nouwen, *In the Name of Jesus: Reflections on Christian Leadership* (New York: Crossroad Publishing, 1989), 64.

15. Rick Warren, "Vulnerability: A Forgotten Virtue of Great Leadership," *Pastors.com*, April 11, 2016, accessed March 4, 2023, https://pastors.com/vulnerability-forgotten-virtue-great-leadership/.

16. Ibid.

CHAPTER 6

Vulnerability in Small Groups

One Sunday after church, I had a lunch appointment with Ethan, a regular attendee of Metro Community Church. Ethan is known for his bold, outspoken nature and sometimes confrontational spirit when engaging with others in the church. Like many of us, Ethan loves being right, sometimes more than being righteous—an inclination I think many of us can relate to. Despite this, Ethan has a genuine love for Jesus and a heart for the least, the last, and the lost. He doesn't just blend in with the crowd; he stands out and is well known by many in our church.

As we were enjoying our lunch, Ethan unexpectedly started tearing up, an uncommon sight in this big, muscular man. I had no idea what had prompted the tears. Initially, I thought he wanted to discuss an idea for reaching more people for Jesus Christ or perhaps provide feedback on my leadership or the general leadership of our church, something he often enjoyed doing. However, I quickly realized that Ethan did not want to meet with me for such trivial matters. Something was deeply bothering him, causing him to cry right in front of me, which was something I had never seen him do before.

He said, "Pastor Peter, I'm turning 40 in a few months, and the truth is, I don't think I have any friends who would want to celebrate with me." Ethan's struggle is a common one that I see with many men as they approach their forties or fifties. We often call this a midlife crisis, but in reality, it's a famine of intimacy that our souls are suffering from. Many men have friends they socialize with, talk about sports, go out for drinks, and have fun. However, men, in general, struggle with loneliness because they lack deep, intimate relationships. For many, the word "intimacy" feels almost derogatory. Men often believe that only women seek intimacy, as our culture has trained us to be warriors, where only the strongest survive.

Ethan had realized that his career wasn't fulfilling his soul's craving for intimacy. At the age of thirty-nine, he found himself questioning whether anyone loved him enough to plan a milestone birthday celebration for him. His tears expressed that there was not a single person.

This realization was profound for Ethan. Despite being surrounded by people at work and church, he felt isolated and disconnected. He admitted that while he had acquaintances and colleagues, he lacked genuine friends who truly knew him and cared for him on a deeper level. Ethan's vulnerability at that moment was a stark contrast to the persona he usually projected—strong, confident, and unshakeable.

Although Ethan had been attending Metro for some time, he hadn't been intentional about building a close, soul mate relationship with another Christian brother in our church. He also admitted that during small group meetings, he often flaunted his knowledge of the Bible and his opinions about Christianity and spiritual life. I thanked Ethan for his honesty with me, but I encouraged him to be equally open and vulnerable in his small group. Additionally, I challenged him to seek out a soul mate within our church community.

Three months later, Ethan stopped me in the hallways of the church and shared that he had found a soul mate and it had been going great. He shared how he and his soul mate were going to travel together to celebrate his 40th birthday. I asked him how he was able to find a soul mate so quickly. Ethan responded, "he is in my small group. I started to be more vulnerable with the group and we just kind of hit it off!" It brings me great joy to see what happens when people find the courage to be vulnerable. The organic nature of finding intimacy is so beautiful.

David HoSang, one of Metro Community Church's esteemed pastors and one of my mentors, often says, "we were created for community." By this, he means that we are designed for intimacy. God created humankind in a way that not only allows us, but requires us, to enter into an intimate relationship with Him and others. Small groups are pathways through which we can begin to live in intimate relationships. Vulnerability in a small group setting allows individuals to form deeper and more transparent relationships.

However, the idea of being vulnerable is met with resistance, not just in the world, but also within the Church. We have a natural inclination to fight against being vulnerable. Christians have no problem admitting that we live in a fallen and broken world, but when it comes to ourselves, we despise admitting that we are broken and weak. As a result, when Christians gather in small groups, they will often put up a type of "guard." This is often perpetuated by the small group leader or facilitator. They have no intention sharing with the group their own struggles in life, and unfortunately, the group follows their lead. When prompted by the small group leader to respond to a particularly personal question or to share a prayer request, Christians will rarely answer in a genuine way. They will often respond with a surface-level comment instead of responding from the depths of their struggling souls. They may even lie and give false answers. Oftentimes, this is the result of individuals not feeling safe in a small group. Reid Smith, a pastor of small groups, emphatically writes that:

> One of the reasons group members complain of a group not being "deep enough" is not so much due to shallow curriculum, as it is the lack of relational depth among participants. The vulnerability that flows from authenticity deepens relationships and results in group discussions that have more depth and challenge to them. There is no greater influence on the dynamic of a group than how real the leader is with the participants. Authenticity is contagious! A leader who is transparent will inspire others to be more real with each other, and consequently, group members will look forward to getting together with more enthusiasm than you might have thought possible![1]

In a Strong Church, people gather as a small group to learn the Bible or other specifically felt needs. The small groups become a microcosm of how preaching is done on the pulpit. The community may have fun and learn God's word together, but seldom do people feel empowered to share their struggles in life for fear of judgment from others. As a result, small groups in a Strong Church are usually shallow and desperately lacking in depth. Carter Moss's article, *5 Mistakes that Ruin Small Groups*, outlines the five key areas that will make a small group struggle and eventually die. They are listed in order of importance: *(1) Allowing an unsafe environment. (2) Moving at the wrong speed. (3) Getting together only for meetings. (4) Killing the group discussion. (5) Sticking together too long.*[2] Moss believes that nothing will ruin a small group more quickly than an environment that feels too unsafe for people to honestly share their struggles. "For small groups to be as impactful in people's lives, the conversations must move below the surface into deeper sharing. This allows the relationships to grow in authenticity. But this absolutely cannot happen if the group is unsafe. If it's not safe to share—people won't."[3] The unfortunate result of this is that, according to Springtide Research, 85 percent of people from the ages of twelve to twenty-five do not see their church as a place to which they can turn when struggling.[4] If churches do not make the shift from being "strong" to "weak," then, as the statistics show, we will be unable to reach the next generation. A Strong Church paradigm only perpetuates this idea that people must only share their own successes and highlights.

Due to the vulnerable nature of the preaching in a Weak Church, the congregation is now empowered to also reflect that same transparency in their own small groups. The small group leader(s) lead the way by being vulnerable themselves. This environment of openness and unconditional acceptance allows the members of the small group community to experience God's power, care, and love.

Mandy Smith is the lead pastor of University Christian Church in Cincinnati, Ohio. In her book, *The Vulnerable Pastor*, she has chosen the Weak Church ministry philosophy. Her book outlines three key areas that pastors and church leaders must develop in order to become a vulnerable pastor: (1) Getting over ourselves, which is vulnerability with God. (2) Being true to ourselves, which is being vulnerable behind the scenes. (3) Practicing in Public, which is being vulnerable with an audience. The church is better at reflecting the world values as opposed to the values of Jesus Christ. Smith argues that because our culture encourages this avoidance of weakness that so many people forget it is even an act. It has become a natural part of life. She states that the only way to challenge this cultural norm of avoiding weakness in any social setting is to learn to confess our weakness and struggles in life with fellow Christians. In our efforts to project strength, we continue a cycle of "unhealthy ideals, setting up unrealistic expectations for others, reproducing something hollow. When we hear only about the strengths and success of others, it crushes us, and in turn, we crush others by presenting only our own strengths and successes. God doesn't need our perfection. He already has His own. He chooses us because we offer something different—humanity."[5] If small groups consist of people living in the world, then one of their preconceived notions is that they need to share their strong selves, rather than their weak vulnerable selves.

A Weak Church empowers its people to be vulnerable in their small groups. Mandy Smith preaches by way of confessing her vulnerable self on the pulpit. She states that "it began with confession to my congregation, with my need to break out of the silent shame of my limitations. . . . I confess that I am vulnerable. Not simply that I feel vulnerable, but that I am inherently susceptible to weakness, inadequacy. In confessing for my own sake, I've watched how it's given grace to others, how it's breaking a culture of performance, perfectionism and shame."[6] A pastor's own vulnerability on the pulpit empowers the small groups to become a safe place for vulnerability. Through this vulnerability, and the subsequent support, the small group community will experience God's power, care, and love. When this happens, vulnerability grows organically, without the need for the small group facilitator to force it upon his or her members. Nevertheless, the small group leader should be willing to set the tone for the group by being vulnerable and authentic first. Reid Smith addresses the challenges of moving a small group from "strong" to "weak." He argues that the most effective way for this to happen is for the small group leader to "open up" and be vulnerable first. By demonstrating vulnerability, the small group leader disrupts the cycle that traps us in our quest for perfection. He or she gives us permission to share our fears, creating a space for others to be human and for God to be God.[7] Peter Scazzero shares the fruits of his vulnerable preaching at New Life Fellowship Church, "One of the outstanding qualities of New Life Fellowship Church today is that leaders freely share their weakness. Ministry and small group leaders, as well as board members and volunteers, are encouraged to tell their stories of weakness and failure as they lead others. . . . As go the leaders, so goes the church."[8]

When a congregation does not embrace a Weak Church philosophy, most of its church congregation will live in isolation. This is not part of God's design for us as He created us to be in community. Dr. Curt Thompson, a psychiatrist, writes that our need for community isn't just theology—its human biology. He contends that our "brain doesn't function well alone. . . . After years of research and clinical practice. I've come to believe everything we ask for and long for in the world is proxy for relationship. Our suffering is mostly . . . isolation."[9] How then can we care for one another if we are clueless as to what is really going on in each other's lives? The church was formed so that the deepest level of care, support, and love would exist among its people (Acts 2:42–47). However, this cannot happen if we are not willing to be vulnerable with one another. Kevin Butcher, in his book *Free*, writes the tragic reality that few Christians see themselves as someone that God is deeply in love with. Rather, the Christian's walk with Jesus Christ is full of duty, fear, and shame. So many Christians are not only discouraged, but he argues that many have "checked out" of the Christian faith. Butcher argues that the only way to break free from a Christian faith that is burdened with duty, fear, and shame is to learn to live in a vulnerable community. "We need the community of Jesus. We need the people in whom Jesus dwells. We need a lifetime of intimate, authentic connection with other sons and daughters of God. To abide, we don't just need Christ—we desperately need the body of Christ."[10] Vulnerability in small groups shouldn't even be an option; it should be the standard. Yes, Bible study is important, and yes, having fun is too, but until the body of Christ can become a place in which people truly feel safe being their most vulnerable selves, the church will just be another social or country club.

To foster an environment where individuals feel empowered to share openly in small groups, ministry teams, or other community gatherings within the church, it is crucial for pastors to adopt an incarnational approach to their preaching. This method, where pastors embody the message they preach, can initiate a ripple effect that encourages a culture of embracing vulnerability and weaknesses. When pastors demonstrate the courage to acknowledge their own weaknesses from the pulpit, it sets a powerful example for the congregation. This authenticity can inspire others within the church to feel more comfortable and empowered to share their own struggles and vulnerabilities, ultimately fostering a more supportive and open community.

By embracing an incarnational preaching approach, pastors not only model transparency and humility but also create a culture where members can connect on a deeper, more genuine level. This approach can transform the church community into a place of mutual support, understanding, and growth, where everyone feels valued and accepted despite their imperfections.

Building and sustaining community are best achieved through the formation of deep, intimate relationships rather than superficial ones. This process fosters genuine connections among people, creating a supportive network where individuals feel valued and understood. God created us with a fundamental need for intimacy, allowing us to share our sadness, fears, doubts, anger, joys, hopes, and dreams freely with others. These authentic connections enable us to navigate life's challenges together, offering mutual support and encouragement.

Without such meaningful relationships, we may wander through life feeling isolated and struggling with the profound impact of loneliness. Loneliness can have detrimental effects on both our mental and physical health, making the presence of close, intimate relationships even more critical. When we lack people with whom we can be vulnerable and honest, we risk feeling disconnected and adrift.

Pastors and church leaders, I understand that being vulnerable as you lead your church comes at a significant cost. However, it is a sacrifice well worth the suffering it may entail. A church that embraces its weaknesses holds immense promise for the future, but this vision can only be realized if pastors and leaders are willing to pick up their cross and follow Jesus into a life of vulnerability. By doing so, they set a powerful example for their congregations, encouraging openness, authenticity, and deep, meaningful connections within the church community. This willingness to embrace and share our own weaknesses is essential for fostering a supportive and resilient church that can truly reflect the love and compassion of Christ.

The Nuts and Bolts of Understanding the Layers of Vulnerability in a Small Group

One might assume that being part of a small group eliminates the need for a soul mate, but this couldn't be further from the truth. The level of vulnerability you experience in a small group is quite different from that shared with a soul mate. The essence of having a soul mate is to engage in a profound level of honesty about your inner struggles, including your sinful nature. With a soul mate, there are no filters; you openly discuss every aspect of your life—the good, the bad, and the ugly.

In contrast, the role of a small group is not to serve as a confessional space for your deepest sins. Rather, a small group is designed to be a supportive, safe community where members can share and support each other through current challenges. It provides a space to discuss day-to-day struggles and offer encouragement, but it is not the ideal setting for addressing the darkest or most personal issues, especially if the group consist of men and women.

For instance, if someone is grappling with issues like pornography or thoughts of adultery, these topics are often too intense and personal to be discussed in a small group setting. Such deep personal struggles are better suited for one-on-one discussions, which allow for a more focused and intimate conversation that a small group setting cannot always accommodate. In a small group, discussing these issues might inadvertently dominate the conversation and detract from the group's overall purpose.

Thus, while small groups offer essential support and community, sharing the most profound and intimate struggles is crucial in a relationship with a soul mate, where complete vulnerability can be met with forgiveness, understanding, and personal guidance.

In a small group setting, the level of sharing should focus on real, yet manageable challenges that you face, without dominating the group's time. These are typically more general struggles rather than highly specific or deeply personal issues. The aim is to foster a supportive environment where everyone feels empowered to share openly and receive support without any single person's issues overwhelming the group dynamic.

For instance, you might share challenges at work, such as difficulties in getting along with a boss or coworker. Similarly, you could open up about general marital struggles without delving into the intricate details of your relationship issues. These kinds of discussions help in creating a safe space for collective support and prayer while keeping the focus on issues that are relevant to the group as a whole.

In a small group, this level of openness ensures that everyone has the opportunity to share and support one another. This way, the group can address important topics without any single personal issue overwhelming the collective group time and focus.

What I've discovered is that people often have an intuitive sense of how to navigate these dynamics. This understanding doesn't need to be explicitly taught before small groups begin meeting. Typically, the level of vulnerability that is appropriate to share in small groups reflects the tone set by the pastor's sermons on Sundays.

When a pastor engages in incarnational preaching—sharing their own struggles and experiences from the pulpit—it sets a precedent for the kind of intimacy and openness that can be mirrored within small groups. This approach helps to create a church environment where individuals feel more empowered to share openly. Consequently, members of the church often feel encouraged to disclose aspects of their lives that they might have hesitated to share in previous group settings. This natural process ensures that while people are more willing to open up, they do so in a manner that respects the group's overall cohesion and purpose.

Several years ago, our small group's pastor approached me with a special request: to conduct a leadership training session for our small group leaders. He said, "Peter, we need you to come up with three hours of material." Initially, I was taken aback. Three hours seemed like an immense amount of time to fill, and I wasn't sure if I had enough content to sustain such a lengthy session. Nevertheless, I accepted the challenge and prepared as thoroughly as I could.

I developed lessons on various topics, including leading a vulnerable small group, teaching the Bible, and multiplying leaders. Despite my preparation, I still doubted whether I had enough material to cover the full three hours. On the day of the training, I decided to start with a simple question to the small group leaders: "How is your small group going?"

To my amazement, each leader began to share deeply personal and vulnerable stories about their groups. They spoke candidly about the extent to which members were opening up and sharing their struggles, fears, and joys. I was profoundly moved by the level of vulnerability and honesty being cultivated in these groups. While I had always believed that incarnational preaching by pastors would naturally lead to openness and vulnerability in small groups, that day provided undeniable proof of this theory in action.

As I listened to their stories, it became clear that the culture of vulnerability within the small groups was a direct result of the pastor's incarnational preaching. When pastors lead by example, embracing their own weaknesses and struggles from the pulpit, it empowers the congregation to do the same. This realization was profound and underscored the importance of authentic leadership in fostering a supportive and open church community.

That day, I ended up deviating from my prepared material. Instead, we immersed ourselves in the culture of vulnerability, allowing the Holy Spirit to guide our time together. The session transformed into a powerful experience of shared openness and mutual support. We spent those hours not just discussing content, but truly living out the principles of vulnerability and authentic community.

This experience reinforced my belief in the transformative power of vulnerability in leadership. It showed me that when pastors and church leaders are willing to share their own struggles and weaknesses, it creates a chain reaction throughout the congregation. It cultivates an environment where everyone feels safe to be their true selves, fostering deeper, more meaningful connections within the church community.

Notes

1. Reid Smith, "5 Ways to Cultivate Vulnerability in Your Small Group," *Lifeway Research*, September 24, 2019, accessed May 4, 2021, https://lifewayresearch.com/2019/09/24/5-ways-to-cultivate-vulnerability-in-your-small-group/.

2. Carter Moss, "5 Mistakes the Ruin Small Groups," Smallgroups.com, February 23, 2015, accessed November 5, 2021, https://www.smallgroups.com/articles/2015/5-mistakes-that-ruin-small-groups.html.

3. Ibid.

4. "Springtide Research," *ROTW.com*, 2021, accessed, December 13, 2021, https://www.rotw.com/get-facts/85-young-people-ages-12-25-don%E2%80%99t-see-their-church-place-they-can-turn-times-trouble.

5. Mandy Smith, *The Vulnerable Pastor* (Downers Grove: Intervarsity Press, 2015), 13.

6. Ibid., 14.

7. Smith, "5 Ways to Cultivate Vulnerability in Your Small Groups."

8. Scazzero, *Emotionally Healthy Discipleship*, 202.

9. Dr. Curt Thompson, *New Canaan Society National Conference* (Championsgate, Florida: Omni Orlando Resort, March 1–3, 2019), accessed December 13, 2021, https://www.youtube.com/watch?v=6J6i-pSQGqc.

10. Butcher, *Free*, 126.

~

CHAPTER 7

Leadership Development

An organization is only as good as its leaders and its ability to develop new leaders. In a church setting that relies heavily on volunteerism, a solid leadership development model is essential in order for a church to be effective in ministering to its parishioners and reaching people outside their church walls. It would be hard to imagine God leading new people to a congregation in which good leadership and leadership development are lacking.

In a Strong Church, leadership development is often in a structured classroom setting through a curriculum that focuses on cognitive learning. Individuals learn how to study and teach the bible, pray, evangelize, and so on. While this is good at some levels, it is insufficient because people—and especially young people—struggle to effectively learn in a classroom format. When leadership development is implemented exclusively in a classroom format, it will eventually become ineffective.

Dr. Eileen Linnaberry makes a strong case that leadership development fails when organizations focus exclusively on a classroom format. Leaders aren't born, they are developed, and if leaders can be developed, Linnaberry questions how it is that organizations fail to develop leaders. She writes that the three reasons why organizations fail to develop leaders are (1) the program focuses too heavily on classroom training; (2) the program lacks momentum; and (3) methods for measuring the program's success are incomplete.

In all our work with leaders, no one has ever told us that a "training program was the most impactful development experience of my career." And yet, classroom training is the most common form of development. Although learning concepts in the classroom may produce short-lived behavioral change, participants often revert to old behaviors over time. To make matters worse, some organizations host so many required classroom trainings that they breed a culture of "I'm only developing when I attend a course" mindset, and inadvertently undervalue learning that happens in the day-to-day. Classroom training becomes the easy trigger to pull any time employees are required to change, but not all change benefits from lectures and theories.[1]

Strong churches, much like corporate America, often rely heavily on a classroom format for leadership development. However, according to Linnaberry, this is a significant oversight because it's been proven that organizations cannot cultivate effective leaders solely through classroom instruction. The Leadership Network echoes this sentiment, emphasizing that the most impactful leadership development happens outside the classroom. They assert that "great churches in leadership development realize that formal classroom content plays a small part in developing leaders."[2] In fact, they suggest that classroom content should constitute no more than 10 percent of an individual's development.

If this holds true, then a staggering 90 percent of leadership development must occur outside the traditional classroom setting. This insight calls for a radical shift in how leadership development is approached in many churches, moving toward more experiential, life-on-life opportunities.

As established in chapter 2, the purpose of embracing weakness and vulnerability is to access God's perfect strength. God's power is revealed through our weakness. Jesus reminded Paul of this essential truth, which became the cornerstone of his leadership: "My grace is sufficient for you, for my power is made perfect in weakness. Therefore I will boast all the more gladly about my weaknesses, so that Christ's power may rest on me."[3]

Every Christian leader needs a moment of realization, like Paul did with the Lord, to understand that effective leadership relies on God's strength. Without it, we cannot lead effectively because God's power is ever-present in our weakness. By embracing our vulnerabilities, we allow Christ's power to work through us, creating a community that truly embodies the strength of God in its collective weakness.

In a Weak Church, leadership development must prioritize teaching future leaders to embrace vulnerability. However, this is a monumental challenge because the Church has naturally adapted to the strength-based patterns of the world in which it exists. Theologian Frederick Dale Bruner describes our strength-based world as "a major social spiritual disease and a principal source of false faith."[4] This deeply ingrained mindset presents a significant barrier to fostering the kind of authentic, vulnerable leadership that a Weak Church aims to cultivate. Scazzero further states that:

We live in a larger culture that believes bigger is always better—bigger profits, bigger influence, bigger impact. And the church more or less believes the same thing. We measure success by the numbers, and bigger is always the goal. . . . Our success-ism drives us to make misguided decisions and to treat people in ways antithetical to the heart of Jesus. At least 90 percent of pastors and leaders I speak with, young and old alike, experience an ironic consequence of success-ism. They feel like failures. Underperformers. Subpar representatives of Jesus.[5]

Jim Collins, a leadership professor, author, and speaker, writes, "The great irony is that the animus and personal ambition that often drive people to positions of power stand at odds with the humility required for Level 5 leadership. When you combine that irony with the fact that boards of directors frequently operate under the false belief that they need to hire a larger-than-life, egocentric leader to make an organization great, you can quickly see why Level 5 leaders rarely appear at the top of our institutions."[6] This insight highlights how our culture's obsession with greatness and strength negatively impacts every arena, especially in the corporate world and even the church. The prevalent belief that leadership equates to dominance and egocentrism stands in stark contrast to the humility and selflessness required for truly effective leadership.

The primary goal of leadership development is to liberate disciples of Jesus from the oppressive grip of our culture's fixation on strength and success. The most effective method to achieve this is by embracing our weakness by becoming vulnerable. Scazzero writes, "The pathway Jesus calls us to walk is an intentional move away from greatness-ism to being little or lowly. Jesus said, 'Whoever takes the lowly position of this child is the greatest in the kingdom of heaven' (Matthew 18:4)."[7] By intentionally shifting away from the pursuit of greatness and adopting a posture of humility and vulnerability, leaders can foster a more authentic and spiritually grounded community.

The Essence of the Life-on-Life Leadership Development

To truly embody the principles of a weak church, a congregation must implement a life-on-life (LOL) leadership development model that fosters a safe and compassionate environment for the candid sharing of life stories. This approach transcends the traditional classroom format that focuses solely on disseminating leadership content. Instead, it delves into the entirety of an individual's life story, spanning from birth to the present, segmented into five-year periods.

During each session, participants share the significant moments of their lives, including the difficult and potentially devastating experiences they may have previously concealed. This process often becomes a form of life confession within the group. The leader or pastor facilitating the session sets the tone of vulnerability by sharing first. This establishes a precedent for openness and honesty.

Each meeting typically features a brief time of teaching followed by one or two individuals sharing their life stories, ensuring ample time for each person. In each meeting, the primary focus is on the life stories being shared, not on the lessons being taught by the pastor or leader. After the sharing, the group engages in a time of affirmation, where members highlight aspects of the shared story that resonated with them. This affirmation is not intended to provide solutions or advice but to offer encouragement, compassion, and understanding. The objective is to help individuals release any shame they may have been carrying, transforming their hidden struggles into profound encounters with God's grace.

The sharing session concludes with a prayer, as the group gathers around the person who shared, offering blessings and encouragement. This practice taps into a divine power that supports and uplifts the individual. As members share their full life stories, they often experience a profound sense of liberation and strength, no longer feeling the need to live in secrecy. Instead, they are empowered by the newfound freedom and the deepened connection with God's grace that this vulnerability fosters.

The Story of Noah

Noah hesitated at first when invited to join my six-month LOL group. He carefully reviewed the requirements, one of which struck a nerve: he had to share his life story. Initially reluctant, Noah eventually agreed to participate despite his reservations. At each meeting, he expressed his apprehension about revealing his life story. It was clear that he carried a heavy burden—a sin he deemed unforgivable, one that had haunted him since his college days, now decades in the past. This sin was something that he had never shared with anyone before.

As Noah, now in his forties, grappled with his inner turmoil, my curiosity deepened. What could this sin be, so weighty that he believed it beyond God's forgiveness? My mind wandered through a spectrum of possibilities, imagining the darkest scenarios—a grave transgression, a crime committed, or someone deeply hurt.

The group, too, became increasingly intrigued and empathetic toward Noah's struggle. Each meeting, we awaited with bated breath for him to share his story, sensing the profound impact it could have on him and us as a group. Finally, the moment arrived. With trembling voice and tears in his eyes, Noah confessed that his unforgivable sin was using part of the tuition money his parents had sacrificed to provide, to gamble at a casino.

The revelation, to some, seemed anticlimactic. Internally, I couldn't help but feel a mixture of surprise and disbelief. "That's it?" I thought incredulously. "That's the unforgivable sin? Are you kidding me?" Yet, as Noah continued to speak, it became clear that the shame and guilt he had carried for nearly two decades were indeed profound and real.

Then, a breakthrough. During the time of affirmation of Noah's story, one of our group members, moved to tears, spoke out passionately: "Noah, this sin does not define you! It does not define you!" Her words cut through the tension and shame, offering a glimpse of grace and acceptance. Noah, overwhelmed by this unexpected outpouring of compassion, broke down. In that moment, the room filled with a palpable sense of empathy and the power of the Holy Spirit.

In the aftermath of Noah's confession, our group experienced a transformation. I realized once again the power of creating safe spaces where people could share vulnerably without judgment. Noah, too, underwent a profound change. Freed from the shackles of guilt and shame, he began to embrace the mercy and grace that had eluded him for so long.

That day marked a turning point for Noah. No longer burdened by his past, he emerged stronger and more resilient. His journey taught us all a valuable lesson: true leadership stems not from perfection, but from authenticity and the willingness to confront and grow from our mistakes. Noah's story became a testament to the transformative power of forgiveness and the healing that comes from community and compassion.

The Vulnerability Loop

Daniel Coyle coined the phrase "the vulnerability loop." A vulnerability loop is a shared exchange of openness. Coyle says that there are five steps to the vulnerability loop:

1. Person A sends a signal of vulnerability.
2. Person B detects this signal.
3. Person B responds by signaling their own vulnerability.
4. Person A detects this signal.
5. A norm is established; closeness and trust increase.[8]

According to Coyle, when a group encounters a vulnerability loop, it transforms the dynamics of how the group will relate to one another. "You can actually see the people relax and connect and start to trust. The group picks up the idea and says, 'Okay, this is the mode we're going to be in,' and it starts behaving along those lines, according to the norm that it's okay to admit weakness and help each other."[9] When leadership development consists of people sharing their life stories, it creates a vulnerability loop that encourages others to share with that same level of openness. This will enable these leaders or future leaders to bring this level of vulnerability to whatever ministry they end up leading in the church.

When we do not share our stories, especially the parts that bring us the greatest level of shame, we will go on leading out of a false self, an imposter that often is incapable of leading effectively. Brené Brown writes that "we need to honor our struggle by sharing it with someone who has earned the right to hear it. . . . The most dangerous thing to do after a shaming experience is hide or bury our story. When we bury our story, the shame metastasizes. . . . We have to own our story and share it with someone who has earned the right to hear it, someone whom we can count on to respond with compassion."[10]

When individuals can openly share their full story, they encounter the purest form of God's strength, which is His grace. They no longer feel the need to hide their stories away. They are able to minister as "weak" leaders who truly reach others through their places of weakness. Pema Chödrön, an American Buddhist nun, boldly declares that only "when we know our own darkness well can we be present with the darkness of others. Compassion becomes real when we recognize our shared humanity."[11] Rob Reimer, a professor, author, and speaker, shares his own testimony of what happens when he participates in a life confession: "It is a liberating feeling to get up in the morning, look yourself in the mirror, and know that you have no secrets. There are no skeletons in the closet; no one is going to accuse you of something that you have not already told another. It's powerful. . . . The enemy of our souls makes honesty terrifying and secrets appealing, but only as we walk in the light with God and others can we truly get free."[12]

While it is important to teach the nuts and bolts of leadership, what must be prioritized is the importance of creating a safe and compassionate environment. This is what will ultimately create a vulnerable and transparent community. Individuals must be encouraged to share the secrets that they have been carrying with them for way too long. Until a leader can become vulnerable, he or she will be ineffective in a Weak Church. The greatest leaders are the ones who have chosen to live in intimate relationships with a small group of people. When they are able to do that, they can truly "own" their stories. In turn, they no longer feel the need to hustle for their worth. It is a biological fact that we, humans, are wired for connection. "From the time we are born, we need connection to thrive emotionally, physically, spiritually, and intellectually. . . . Our innate need for connection makes the consequences of disconnection that much more real and dangerous."[13] Dr. Daniel Goleman learned in his research that "even our most routine encounters act as regulators in the brain priming our emotions, some desirable, others not. The more strongly connected we are with someone emotionally, the greater the mutual force."[14]

There is a myriad of leadership development models out there, but if a church desires to minister out of its weakness, it must teach and develop its leaders to become vulnerable. When leaders-in-training share life stories that include not only their "wow" moments, but also their "woe" moments, they are able to encounter God's perfect strength. They evolve into mighty and Godly leaders who have no problem being vulnerable with the people they lead because they are fully aware that they have access to God's perfect strength.

A significant part of leadership development then is helping individuals confront and deal with their shame. By addressing this deep-seated issue, people can begin to see their weaknesses not as flaws but as unique strengths or superpowers. The goal isn't to eradicate our weaknesses but to overcome the shame associated with them.

Shame can be a powerful and debilitating emotion that hinders personal and professional growth. It can prevent individuals from taking risks, embracing new opportunities, and fully utilizing their potential. The path to overcoming shame begins with vulnerability. By opening up and sharing our experiences of shame with others, we create a space for healing and connection.

In leadership development, fostering an environment of trust and openness is crucial. Leaders must model vulnerability, demonstrating that it is not a sign of weakness but a strength. When leaders share their struggles and how they have dealt with shame, it encourages others to do the same.

This process of sharing and vulnerability helps to normalize the experience of shame, making it less of a burden. It also allows individuals to receive support, empathy, and encouragement from others, which can be incredibly empowering.

Therefore, the chief task of leadership development is to guide people through this journey of overcoming shame. By doing so, we enable them to unlock their full potential and lead with authenticity and confidence. This transformation not only benefits the individual but also strengthens the entire church, creating a culture of resilience and mutual support.

The Nuts and Bolts of LOL Leadership Development Group

Over the years, pastors have asked me for my material for how I develop leaders. I believe that there is a scarcity of resources out there that deviates from the traditional classroom format. Rather than share everything that I do, because I am a firm believer that one size does not fit all, let me go over the key components of LOL leadership groups.

1. Duration

   LOL groups should last at least six months, though they can extend up to a year if needed. Leading an LOL group requires significant time and dedication from the pastor or church leader. If you feel hesitant about the time commitment, remember that Jesus discipled people amid his busy schedule. One of the most important roles of a pastor, especially a senior or lead pastor, is to disciple and raise up leaders. By doing so, we are truly imitating Jesus Christ.

2. Invitation Only

   LOL groups should never be volunteer-based; participation must be by invitation only. These are the individuals whom God has placed on the pastor or church leader's heart. The pastor or church leader should have no more than twelve people in the group. I usually invite about fifteen and let them know that I will accept the first twelve who respond. This approach encourages a prompt response rather than waiting until the last minute. I prefer to invite those who are not already leading any ministries within the church. I look for individuals who demonstrate leadership potential, but I also extend invitations to those who might never be asked to join a leadership group. These are people who are often on the fringe of the church. The goal is to take chances on people, much like Jesus did with the twelve. If pastors and church leaders only select those who are rising stars and demonstrate strength, it contradicts the philosophy of ministering out of our weakness.

   Remember what Jesus said about the woman who anointed his feet with her tears and expensive perfume: "Therefore, I tell you, her many sins have been forgiven—as her great love has shown. But whoever has been forgiven little loves little."[15] This profound statement reveals a deep truth about forgiveness and love. Those who have been forgiven much, love much. Their capacity to love is magnified because they understand the depths of grace and mercy they have received.

Pastors and church leaders should take chances on people who have been forgiven much because, in the end, they possess a greater capacity to love than those who have been forgiven little. By embracing and empowering these individuals, leaders can cultivate a community rich in empathy, compassion, and profound love.

Once you have your list of people you'd like to invite, write each of them a personal invitation letter. In the letter, be sure to include:

- The reason you have chosen them to be in your group.
- What they can expect to gain from participating in the group.
- Your expectations upon their completion of LOL group. I make it clear that they will be expected to lead a ministry in the church. If I am committing to invest six months into their lives, they in return will take on a leadership role within the church.
- The dates and times of each meeting. I allow only two excused absences.
- A requirement to become a member of the church if they are not already.
- A commitment to begin tithing to the church.
- Permission for you to speak truth into their lives.

3. Topics to Cover

Over the six-month span, I typically meet with the LOL group between sixteen and eighteen times, averaging about three meetings a month.

In our first meeting, I establish an **open-door policy** to my home. I tell the group that for the next six months, my house is their house. They are welcome to come over anytime, join us for meals, and eat with my family. If they want to cook dinner for us, they can come over every day! It's important for them to see how I live with my family. I even invite them to sleep over or live with us for a time if they wish. I firmly believe that people learn more about following Jesus by observing how I live rather than from what I teach on Sundays or in workshops. The group members love this and take full advantage of coming over.

I realize this might be a big ask of a pastor and their family. However, Jenny and I genuinely enjoy hosting, and our children do too. While it is a significant commitment, we believe it's a worthwhile sacrifice. Remember, you're not inviting everyone from the church—just the group you're investing in and nurturing as future leaders.

One evening, Don came over for dinner, marking his fifth visit to our home. My kids adored him, especially my son Christian, who enjoyed playing with him. However, this time, Jenny and I had a disagreement during the meal, and the atmosphere grew tense. Don seemed quite uncomfortable, so I asked, "Don, would you mind watching the kids while Jenny and I step aside to talk things through?" He looked visibly relieved and quickly agreed, saying, "Yes! Please, take all the time you need."

Jenny and I retreated to our bedroom to work out our issues. When we came back, I filled Don in on what had happened and how we resolved it. I felt a sense of pride that evening for not shying away from the argument or waiting until Don left. I wanted him to witness a typical day in our home, and he certainly did. Don saw both our weaknesses and how we addressed them, providing him with a real-life example of conflict resolution—something especially valuable for him as a newlywed.

When choosing topics for your LOL group, I encourage pastors and church leaders to focus on themes they hope group members will continue to embrace after the group concludes. I often advise, "Start with the end in mind" when leading a LOL group. Keep in mind that teachings should be secondary and limited to a maximum of thirty minutes. The majority of the group time should be dedicated to sharing personal stories. Here are some topic suggestions:

- Weakology
- Soul Mate
- Silence and Solitude
- Sabbath
- Tithing
- Soul Care by Rob Reimer
- Praying
- *Emotionally Healthy Spirituality* by Peter Scazzero
- Meditating on Scripture

4. Two One-on-One Meetings

Connecting with your LOL group members on a one-on-one basis is crucial for their development. This step cannot be overlooked. The first meeting should take place probably within the first month. The last meeting should happen toward the end of the six months.

First Meeting

In the first meeting, the people are responsible to come prepared to give you a copy of their life line that you tell them ahead of time to prepare.

Life Line Exercise Instructions
For the Mentee:

1. **Draw Your Life Line:**
   - Start by drawing a horizontal line that represents your life, beginning from 0 (your birth) to your current age.
   - Divide this line into five-year segments.

   0 ————————————————————————————— Current Age

2. **Mark Significant Moments:**
   - For each five-year segment, jot down significant moments from your life. Include both positive experiences and challenges.
   - Consider major events, achievements, and any difficulties or obstacles you have faced.

For the Mentor:

1. **Reflect and Ask Questions:**
   - This exercise is essential because it uncovers the key narratives that shape the person's life.
   - Pay special attention to particularly difficult periods.
   - Be ready to ask questions to gain a clearer understanding of their past, which will help guide your mentorship and strategic planning for the next meeting.

2. **Prepare for Group Sharing:**
   - When a mentee first shares their life story with their mentor, it helps them feel more prepared and confident to share it with the group when their turn comes.
   - Make sure to explain to the mentee that the life line serves as an outline for the life story they will write and share with the group.

3. **Create a Legacy:**
   - Let the mentee know that their life story can be developed into a memoir to share with their children, future children, or grandchildren.

- This document can become a cherished legacy—something they may wish they had received from their own parents or grandparents.
- Encourage the group to update their life stories every five years, capturing both the high and low points from that time.

As members of your LOL group begin writing their life stories, encourage them to invite the Holy Spirit into the process. For many, this may be the first time they've revisited some of the most challenging and painful moments of their lives. Remind them that by welcoming the Holy Spirit, they are not simply recounting events but opening their hearts to the healing and comforting presence of Jesus Christ. This act of surrender can bring new insights, peace, and a deeper sense of God's love and grace in their journey.

Eddie was often bullied in school, with kids mocking him because of his crooked teeth. The constant name-calling was unbearable, driving his already low self-esteem to rock bottom. He dreaded going to school. During his high school years, the bullying intensified. Classmates would throw spitballs at him, provoking laughter from the entire class. Eddie felt humiliated and demoralized. He longed to fight back, but his fear of standing up for himself was greater than his anger. He felt like a coward, incapable of defending himself. Even as an adult, he frequently revisited his childhood trauma whenever he was put in situations where he was unable to stick up for himself.

However, as Eddie wrote out his life story and detailed his years of being bullied, something wonderful happened. The Holy Spirit spoke to him as he described his inability to fight back, especially during the spitball incidents. The Holy Spirit said, "Eddie, you were never more like Jesus when you didn't retaliate. Jesus never fought back when he was beaten and tortured." These words were deeply healing for Eddie—words he never thought he would hear. In his late forties, Eddie had spent his entire life feeling like a coward, but while writing his life line, he realized through the Holy Spirit that he had never been more like Jesus. He experienced profound healing.

When Eddie shared his life story with the group, we could sense the redemption he had experienced through writing his life story. There was an excitement and energy as he recounted the years of being bullied. Hope had taken root in Eddie, and he would never be the same again. His encounter with God while writing his life story was a defining moment—one that would never be forgotten and, more importantly, one that freed him from the tyranny of negativity that had plagued him for so much of his life.

Second Meeting

In the final meeting, the pastor or church leader will explore the possibilities and consequences of each mentee's life. The best approach is to write a strategic life plan. With their life line, life story, and observations from the past six months of interactions in the LOL group, you have a comprehensive understanding of each person. This includes their strengths and areas for growth, which you have seen in various settings, including at your home.

The strategic plan serves multiple purposes. It helps define reality for the individual, highlighting what makes them special and identifying areas where they can grow. Additionally, it provides a clear, actionable plan for personal development based on your insights and observations. Lastly, the strategic plan places them in a ministry for them to lead at the church.

Two-Night Three-Day Retreat

At the two-to-three-month mark, the LOL group goes on a retreat. This retreat is a pivotal moment in our journey together, and it's best to rent a house where the entire group can stay under one roof. Living together in a shared space fosters deeper relationships and a stronger sense of community that can't be achieved in our regular meetings alone.

During the retreat, we engage in various activities designed to build trust and camaraderie. We share meals, worship together, play games, and have extended times of prayer and reflection. These shared experiences create opportunities for vulnerability and open communication, allowing group members to connect on a deeper level.

There is something uniquely powerful about stepping away from our daily routines and immersing ourselves in a communal environment. Without the distractions of everyday life, the group can focus entirely on their relationships with each other and with God.

This retreat is more than just a getaway; it is a transformative experience that leaves a lasting impact on everyone involved. The bonds formed and the spiritual growth experienced during this time are integral to the journey of leadership and personal development that we embark on together.

There are three things that are crucial to cover at the retreat.

1. Sharing of Life Story

Continue to have people share their life story in the group. I usually have about three to four people share their life story at the retreat.

2. Time of Affirmation

On the last night together, dedicate time specifically for affirmation. This practice involves going around the group and having each person take a turn being affirmed by the others. Unfortunately, we live in a world where genuine affirmation is rare. Instead, gossip, criticism, and cyber shaming have become all too common. As a result, intentional affirmation is something we seldom experience in our daily lives.

Creating this space for affirmation is crucial. It allows each person to hear positive, uplifting feedback and to be recognized for their unique qualities and contributions. This intentional practice helps to counteract the negative messages that often permeate our lives and can have a profound impact on an individual's self-esteem and sense of belonging.

During this time, each group member can share specific qualities they appreciate in the person being affirmed. They can recall moments when that person demonstrated kindness, courage, or leadership. This exercise not only boosts the confidence of the individual being affirmed but also strengthens the bonds within the group.

Incorporating affirmation into leadership development is essential. As Hebrews 10:24–25 reminds us, "And let us consider how we may spur one another on toward love and good deeds, not giving up meeting together, as some are in the habit of doing, but encouraging one another—and all the more as you see the Day approaching." Affirmation helps to build a supportive and encouraging community, fostering an environment where individuals can grow and thrive.

The affirmations shared during these times often become unforgettable moments for individuals. They can serve as the impetus for taking greater steps of faith, embracing new challenges, and developing a deeper sense of self-worth. By dedicating time for affirmation, we create a culture of positivity and support that can have lasting effects on each person's journey.

3. Foot Washing

After the affirmation time, we typically move directly into a foot-washing ceremony. This practice is deeply symbolic and rooted in the example set by Jesus. I begin by reading John 13:1–17 where Jesus washes His disciples' feet. This powerful moment serves as a reminder of the humility and servitude that Jesus exemplified.

I explain to the group that this act of foot washing is not just a ritual, but a profound commitment to serving one another. It signifies that we are dedicating ourselves to one another in service and love. We are no longer just acquaintances or even friends; through this act, we acknowledge that we are true brothers and sisters in Christ. This shared experience brings a deep sense of unity and solidarity among us.

As we prepare for the foot washing, I emphasize the importance of approaching this act with a heart of humility and love. It is a time to let go of any barriers or discomfort and embrace the spirit of service. Typically, we follow a general rule of thumb where the men wash each other's feet, and the women do likewise. This helps to maintain a comfortable and respectful environment for everyone involved.

The act of washing each other's feet is transformative. It breaks down walls and fosters a sense of equality and mutual respect. Each person has the opportunity to serve and be served, creating a reciprocal bond of care and commitment. The simple, yet profound act of kneeling before another person and washing their feet echoes the humility and love that Jesus demonstrated.

As we conclude the foot-washing ceremony, the atmosphere is often filled with a sense of peace and unity. We have bonded not just through words of affirmation but through a tangible act of love and service. This experience strengthens the group, reinforcing our identity as a community of believers who are dedicated to supporting and serving each other.

Final Thoughts

When individuals graduate from the LOL group, they emerge as the leaders who will shape and sustain a culture of embracing weakness within the church. These graduates become the curators of vulnerability, demonstrating through their own experiences and growth the power of authentic, humble leadership.

Pastors and church leaders consider the profound impact of this transformation. Is it not worth the time and commitment to invest in these groups? By dedicating your energy and resources to the LOL groups, you are not only fostering the development of individual members but also cultivating a church environment grounded in weakness and mutual support.

The investment you make in these groups pays significant dividends. Graduates of the LOL group become deeply committed to the church and to you as their leader. This loyalty is not superficial; it is a natural outcome of the time and care you have poured into their development. They have experienced firsthand the transformative power of vulnerability and the strength that comes from acknowledging and sharing their weaknesses.

These leaders will be instrumental in nurturing a supportive and weak church culture. Their willingness to be open and honest encourages others to do the same, breaking down barriers and fostering genuine connections within the congregation. They lead by example, showing that true strength lies in vulnerability and that growth comes from embracing our imperfections.

In the end, investing in LOL groups is not just about individual growth; it is about cultivating a church culture that values vulnerability, authenticity, and mutual support. The leaders who emerge from these groups will be the pillars of the church, driving positive change and fostering a community where everyone feels valued and supported. Pastors and church leaders, the time and commitment you invest in these groups will yield lasting benefits, creating a weak, more unified church that truly reflects the love and grace of Christ.

Notes

1. Eileen Linnaberry, "Why Your Leadership Development Program Isn't Working, and What To Do About It," *Vantage Leadership*, 2021, accessed January 21, 2023, https://www.vantageleadership.com/our-blog/leadership-development-programs-not-delivering-results/.

2. "10 Truths of Churches That Do a Great Job With Leadership Development," *Leadnet.org*, June 11, 2019, accessed May 4, 2021, https://leadnet.org/10-truths-of-churches-that-do-a-great-job-with-leadership-development-part-2/.

3. 2 Corinthians 12:9.

4. Fredrick Dale Bruner, *Matthew: A Commentary, Volume 2: The Churchbook, Matthew 13–28* (Grand Rapids: Eerdmans Publishing, 1987), 814.

5. Scazzero, *Emotionally Healthy Discipleship*, 73–74.

6. Jim Collins, *Good to Great* (New York: Harper Collins Publishing, 2001), 36–37.

7. Scazzero, *Emotionally Healthy Discipleship*, 72.

8. Daniel Coyle, "How Showing Vulnerability Helps Build Stronger Teams," *Ideas.Ted.com*, February 20, 2018, accessed January 21, 2023, https://ideas.ted.com/how-showing-vulnerability-helps-build-a-stronger-team/.

9. Ibid.

10. Brown, *The Gifts of Imperfection*, 9–11.

11. Pema Chodron, *The Places That Scare You* (Boston: Shambhala Publication, 2001), 78.

12. Rob Reimer, *Soul Care* (Franklin: Carpenter's Son Publishing, 2016), 84–85.

13. Brown, *The Gifts of Imperfection*, 19–20.

14. Daniel Goleman, *Social Intelligence: The New Science of Human Relationships* (New York: Random House/Bantam Dell, 2006), 38.

15. Luke 7:47.

C H A P T E R   8

~

Deep Compassion for Serving the Poor and Oppressed

The incarnation of Jesus Christ is a profound and beautiful truth for us to contemplate. In an act of unparalleled humility and love, God chose to become weak, entering human history not as a powerful deity, but as a fragile human being. By taking on human flesh, Jesus embraced the limitations and struggles that come with our existence. He walked among us, experiencing our joys and sorrows, our triumphs and trials, so that He could truly understand and relate to our weaknesses.

This act of incarnation is more than just a theological concept; it is the ultimate expression of God's love and passion for His people. Jesus didn't just come to teach or perform miracles; He came to live as one of us, to share in our humanity, and to bridge the gap between the divine and the mortal. His willingness to enter into our world, to suffer and sacrifice for our sake, demonstrates an extraordinary commitment to us. It shows that we are not alone in our struggles, and that God is intimately involved in our lives.

What an awe-inspiring and humbling realization that the Creator of the universe would stoop to our level, to walk in our shoes, and to bear our burdens. The incarnation is a testament to the boundless love and compassion that Jesus has for His people, a love so deep and profound that it defies comprehension.

My mother had made the heart-wrenching decision to leave my father and my sisters and me. It was a choice she felt she had no option but to make, as the physical beatings from my father had become unbearable. Though she didn't want to leave her three young children behind, she had no means to provide for us. Her friend offered her a place to stay, but couldn't accommodate three little kids. So, late in the evening while we were sleeping, my mother packed her bags and prepared to leave us.

93

Her plan was to leave temporarily. She needed time to earn enough money to get her own apartment and then come back for us. Before walking out, she wanted to catch one last glimpse of her three children. In our small two-bedroom apartment, my sisters and I shared a room. As we slept soundly, my mother broke down in tears. She couldn't bring herself to leave us, knowing the pain of growing up without a mother, as she had lost her own mother at a very young age and had no memory of her.

Embracing her weaknesses along with ours, my mother made a very difficult decision. She resolved that no matter what, she would never leave her children behind, no matter how challenging it got with my father.

I can never repay my mother for the depth of her sacrifice. She should have left my father and divorced him, but she didn't because she knew all too well the pain of growing up motherless. She was also terrified of what my father might do to my sisters and me if she were no longer there to protect us from his aggression when he was drunk. Despite the pain that awaited her, she was willing to endure it because of her profound love and unwavering commitment to her vulnerable children.

The Church is called to be an incarnational presence to the poor and oppressed. Ministry to the vulnerable is a command from God Himself. If Christians aspire to be more like Jesus, they must take ministering to the marginalized as seriously as He did. For Jesus, this was not just one of many ministries; it was His mission and the reason God sent Him. "The Spirit of the Lord is on me, because he has anointed me to proclaim good news to the poor. He has sent me to proclaim freedom for the prisoners and recovery of sight for the blind, to set the oppressed free, to proclaim the year of the Lord's favor."[1]

The goal of a Weak Church is not just to help its people embrace their weaknesses so they can flourish and be freed from shame—though that is certainly a powerful transformation. The ultimate goal of a Weak Church goes beyond personal healing and growth; it is to raise up Christians who not only embrace their weakness and lead within the church but also extend love and compassion to those outside the church who are struggling in their brokenness.

Who better to walk alongside the weak and broken than Christians who have fully embraced their own weakness and brokenness? When Christians become vulnerable beings, they are uniquely equipped to demonstrate compassion and minister to the hurting people of this world.

Weak Churches are positioned to have the most profound impact on the least, the last, and the lost because they minister not from a place of superiority or strength, but from their shared brokenness. This deep solidarity creates the foundation for incarnational ministry, where we do not simply serve the poor and oppressed from a distance but walk with them, fully present in their struggles. A Weak Church is not just a refuge for the borken—it is a movement of people who, through their own weakness, become vessels of God's love and healing to the world.

God shows us through scripture that the church has an obligation to the poor. It is inescapable. No matter where we turn to in scripture, we will always find a pericope that addresses the poor. Jim Wallis outlines the frequency in which scripture addresses the poor and oppressed in his article, "Who Is My Neighbor?" In the Old Testament, the subject of the poor is the second most prominent theme. Idolatry is the first, and the two motifs are often connected. In the New Testament, one out of every sixteen verses are about the poor! In the gospels, the number is one out of every ten verses. In Luke's Gospel, this number is one out of every seven, and in the book of James, it is one out of every five verses.[2]

Scripture is completely saturated with the subject of the poor and oppressed. God indisputably has a special love for the poor, the disenfranchised, the marginalized—those who are on the bottom of everybody else's priority list. Ron Sider in his book, *Rich Christians in an Age of Hunger*, dissects the importance of economic equity that God desires for every person and family, at least to the point of having access to the resources that are necessary to live and work responsibly. God has special concern for the poor. There are hundreds of biblical texts that inform God's people that He still measures societies by what God's people do to the poorest of the poor. Sider argues that "God not only acts in history to liberate the poor, the Sovereign of the universe identifies with the weak and destitute. . . . Assisting a poor person is like helping the Creator of all things with a loan."[3] Therefore, God now demands that His Church share God's special concern for the poor. The Bible, however, goes one step further. God insists that if believers do not imitate God's concern for the poor, they are not really God's people regardless of how frequently they may attend church or Bible study. When Israel failed to correct oppression and defend poor widows, Isaiah insisted that Israel was really the pagan people of Gomorrah.[4] God even despised their fasting because they tried to simultaneously worship God and oppress their workers.[5] Jeremiah teaches that knowing God is inseparable from caring for the poor.[6] Jesus drove this message home by declaring that the failure to feed the hungry condemns individuals to hell.[7] John tells us very clearly that if we do not care for the needy brother or sister, then God's love does not reside in us.[8] "Our fidelity to Scripture will not be tested by our dogma and doctrine, but by how our lives demonstrate that we believe that the gospel is good news to the poor."[9]

A Strong Church does not prioritize the needs of the poor and oppressed. Richard Stearns addresses this in his book, *Hole in the Gospel*. He writes that the church is "so preoccupied with their own programs and people that they failed to see the bigger picture. . . . We need only to read our church bulletin to see where our priorities have been placed. How many of the announcements involve programs that focus more on meeting our needs than the needs of those outside the church?"[10] Strong Churches are often so focused on themselves that they forget the importance of serving the poor and oppressed. World Vision conducted a survey of pastors in which they asked pastors to rate the things they considered real priorities for their churches. "79 percent listed worship, 57 percent, evangelism; 55 percent, children's ministry; and 47 percent, discipleship programs. Just 18 percent said that 'helping the poor and disadvantaged people overseas' was their 'highest priority.'[11] The church so often forsakes God's way and opts instead for the way of the world."[12]

When a Strong Church does, however, serve the poor and others who are less fortunate, it often does this because it is the noble thing to do. Churches serve the poor and oppressed from the perspective that they are bringing Jesus to them. Outreach of this kind often generates positive feelings of accomplishment in ourselves because we assume the role of the strong giver, while those whom we serve are relegated to the role of the weak recipient who are dependent on our help.

Stephen White in his provocative article, "Why We Need a Church That Is Poor and for the Poor", addresses the importance of church needing to embrace their own poverty if they are able to love and serve the poor the way Jesus exemplifies in the Gospel. God became poor for us in order to enrich humanity with His poverty. If Christ identifies himself with the poor in a special way and became poor himself, how can the church, the body of Christ, do otherwise? "The Church often conceive their obligation to the poor almost exclusively as a function of distribution, of moving goods from those who have to those who have not . . . we must view the poor as more than receptacles for our beneficence, still less that those poorer than ourselves might possess something that we lack and need. Rather than take the risk of being receptive and vulnerable to them, we allow them to remain strangers, alienated and excluded."[13] When the labor of the church on behalf of the poor—our works of mercy—are cut off from the proclamation of Jesus Christ, then the church's work in serving the poor remains sterile, merely human. Pope Francis exclaims: "We can walk as much as we want, we can build many things, but if we do not profess Jesus Christ, things go wrong. We may become a charitable N.G.O., but not the church, the bride of the Lord."[14]

In a Weak Church, serving the poor and oppressed in and outside the church is part of the church's DNA. The congregation serves the marginalized with an awareness of their own brokenness and poverty of spirit, which then fosters solidarity with those to whom they reach out. Furthermore, Weak Church Christians believe that Jesus is among the least, the last, and the lost (Matt. 25:31–46), and therefore, believe that they serve the marginalized, not out of noble obligation, but out of reverence. They believe that it is in serving "the least of these" that they serve and meet Jesus himself. Ron Sider powerfully summarized Matthew 25:31–46 when he wrote, "what does it mean to feed and clothe the Creator of all things? We cannot know. We can only look on the poor and oppressed with new eyes and resolve to heal their hurts and help end their oppression. . . . What does it mean to see the Lord of the universe lying by the roadside starving and walk by on the other side? We cannot know. We can only pledge, in fear and trembling, not to kill him again."[15]

In a Weak Church, serving the least, the last, and the lost is not necessarily an outreach ministry, but rather, it is more importantly an opportunity to grow in our own discipleship. Christians meet Jesus when they serve the hurting people of this world. One of the best ways for us to grow in our faith is by serving Jesus through the *least of these*. If you stare into the eyes of humility, you may sense an eerie awareness that Jesus is staring right back at you!

The Story of Bernice

Bernice is a Mexican American mother of three children who I met at the Door of Hope. For one of my classes in seminary, we had an assignment to do some form of ministry to the poor and write a paper about our experiences. The Door of Hope is a Christian faith-based organization that meets the physical, emotional, and spiritual needs of homeless families with children. Trying to get their life back together, Bernice along with her husband and three children have turned to the Door of Hope for help.

I spent an entire afternoon and most of the evening with the families at the Door of Hope. I was fortunate enough to share a meal with them. As I sat at the dinner table, surrounded by parents and their children, I sensed a real presence of Jesus Christ in our midst. For them, it was just another meal, but for me, it was a moment I would cherish for the rest of my life.

As everyone finished their dinner, Bernice and I were the only ones remaining at the table. We began talking about life, and in a very short time, Bernice started sharing with me the adversities she had endured from childhood to adulthood: sexual, physical, and emotional abuse inflicted by her family. I was shocked to hear her testimony—not just because of the oppression and poverty she had endured throughout her life, but also because she was willing to share such intimate details with me, a stranger.

The most shocking thing I experienced that night was her forgiving heart toward her family and all those who had oppressed her in the past. She proclaimed boldly that because of Jesus' healing and unconditional love, she was able to forgive and even love the ones who had hurt her the most.

When I left the Door of Hope that night, I was convinced I had met Jesus through Bernice. For the first time, I experienced something I had only understood on a cognitive level: God is with the poor and identifies with them in His presence and power, ministering to and through them. I began to feel envious of Bernice's spirituality. The immense love she possessed made me wonder why I wasn't experiencing that kind of love. What allowed Bernice to experience the love of Christ so deeply that she could love her enemies? Why wasn't I experiencing what Bernice was experiencing?

Through this experience, I realized the critical importance of a discipleship that surrounds ourselves with hurting people in this world. At the dinner table, I shared with Bernice my own story of physical abuse by my father. We connected through our shared vulnerabilities, and in that moment, I met Jesus. It was a far deeper encounter than attending a Bible study, prayer meeting, or even church. God is with the poor and oppressed, and if you truly want to meet Jesus through them, you must be willing to minister from your own place of weakness.

Serving the poor and oppressed from our own weaknesses rather than our strengths allows the church and its people to enter into solidarity with those we are serving. In this manner, our love and service come from a place of deep respect. We understand others' pain, losses, and poverty because we, also, are in touch with our own weaknesses. When this happens, God's perfect strength is present for all to experience and encounter. A Weak Church's sense of compassion isn't derived from a place of superiority, rather, it originates from the throes of the Father's heart because His strength is made perfect in our weakness. White suggests that

God became poor to enrich us by His poverty. The option for the poor, then, arises from the very heart of the mission of the church because it is central to the saving mission of Christ. In his love and mercy he treats us, lowly sinners that we are, as though we have something to offer him. He loves us and lets us love him. When we approach the poor and suffering with this same humility, we discover a privileged place of encounter with Christ, who is already there amongst his beloved poor who know and experience his suffering in a special way.[16]

Mother Teresa of Calcutta was a person who dedicated her life to the poor. She was world-renown for the love she had for the poor and oppressed. In her own words Mother Teresa said, "The poor anywhere in the world are Christ who suffers. In them, the Son of God lives and dies. Through them, God shows his face. When we touch the sick and needy, we touch the suffering body of Christ."[17] Mother Teresa saw Jesus Christ in the poor and oppressed. She encourages everyone to do likewise, "We need the eyes of deep faith to see Christ in the broken body and dirty clothes under which the most beautiful One among the sons of the men hides."[18] "How pure our hands must be if we have to touch Christ's Body as the priest touches Him in the appearance of bread at the altar. With what love and devotion and faith he lifts the sacred host! These same feelings we too must have when we lift the body of the sick poor."[19]

We live in a time where many are suffering deeply: people are starving due to lack of food, freezing without shelter, and going without clothing. Some face isolation due to diseases like leprosy, which alienate them from society. This is just a glimpse into the broader issues of poverty and oppression that plague our world.

In the midst of this suffering, there is a powerful call for Christians to respond with compassion and hope. We cannot simply watch as the divide between the rich and poor widens; we are called to take action.

Our mission is to reach out to God's vulnerable children, recognizing our own shared brokenness and weaknesses. When we approach those in need, we do so not from a place of obligation, but from a deep sense of reverence, as if we are in the presence of Jesus Christ Himself. Jesus emphasizes this in Matthew 25:40, where He says that whatever we do for the least of these, we do for Him.

For too long, Christians have lost sight of our shared identity as brothers and sisters, sons and daughters of God. We are bound together by our common destiny, and God desires us to live in unity or face the consequences of forgetting our interconnectedness.

It is time to heed the words of the prophet Amos: "Let justice roll" "into the streets of oppression and drugs and hopelessness, and also into the avenues of luxury and fear. 'Let justice roll' into the ghettos and barrios and squatter camps, but also into the affluent suburbs of comfort and indifference. 'Let justice roll' into the board rooms of corporate wealth and the corridors of political power."[20]

The Nuts and Bolts of a Justice, Advocacy, and Compassion Ministry

Metro Community Church employs a dedicated pastor for our Justice, Advocacy, and Compassion (JAC) ministry. For multi-staff churches, it is crucial to consider hiring a JAC pastor or director. Through our experience, we've learned that a sustainable ministry focused on compassion for the poor and oppressed requires a full-time employee. This role is essential not only for establishing ministry opportunities but also for training the congregation in Metro's unique approach to serving the least, the last, and the lost.

For churches with a solo pastor, it is essential to cultivate and empower lay leaders to assist in overseeing the JAC ministry. As you lead a LOL (Life-on-Life) group, prioritize identifying and developing individuals from this group who can take on leadership roles within the JAC ministry. By investing in these emerging leaders, you not only strengthen the ministry's impact but also build a collaborative team that can support and sustain the church's mission of compassion and justice. This approach ensures that the work of the JAC ministry is shared and grows effectively, even within the constraints of a solo pastorate.

At Metro Community Church, the JAC pastor aims to have every regular attender engage in at least one JAC-related ministry each year. To achieve this, it's crucial to integrate a JAC component into every church ministry. The JAC pastor collaborates with each pastor and ministry director to identify opportunities for their ministries to participate in JAC events. Here are some examples of JAC ministries we've offered over the years:

- Quarterly Prison Ministry at East Jersey State Prison
- Prison Pen Pal Ministry
- Weekly Food Pantry Ministry
- Mentoring At-Risk Youth in Englewood
- Homeless Ministry to Families in Bergen County
- Soup Kitchen
- Back-to-School Block Parties
- Annual Health Day—doctors and nurses in the church administer flu shots and take blood pressure
- *Livin' It Up*, an annual banquet for homeless community in Bergen County
- Metro Life, an after-school program for high school students
- Computer Classes
- ESL

- SAT Classes
- Open Store, a bi-annual free flea market for the underprivileged in Bergen County
- Annual Missions Trip to South Africa and Thailand

Livin' It Up Banquet

One of the most remarkable events hosted by Metro Community Church is our annual banquet for the homeless in Bergen County, NJ. We call this event *Livin' It Up*! We go all out, hiring a wedding band and having chefs prepare a five-star meal. Hundreds of our church members volunteer to make this event a truly unforgettable experience. Our aim is to treat each guest with the dignity and respect they deserve, as if they were billionaires—because in God's eyes, they truly are special.

The evening is filled with joy and celebration. The band plays lively music, encouraging guests to dance the night away, and our photo booth is constantly busy capturing memories. We strive to serve the homeless with unparalleled dignity, which is something they have lost due to their economic circumstances.

I will never forget the moment at one of our *Livin' It Up* events when the band played love ballads, prompting many guests to slow dance with a partner. It was heartwarming to see so many people enjoying the music together, including members of our church who joined in the dancing with our very special guests. As I scanned the room, I noticed a woman who was sitting all by herself. She looked like she wanted to dance, but she didn't have a partner. I noticed that it might be difficult for her to find a dance partner. Her clothes were unkempt, and her hair was disheveled. And when I approached her to ask for a dance, I could smell an uncomfortable odor coming from her. I approached her and asked if she'd like to dance. To my delight, she smiled and agreed.

We danced to a few songs, and as we moved to the music, she said passionately, "I can't believe this!" Initially, I thought she was complementing me on my dancing skills, but soon I realized she was expressing her astonishment at the event itself. She shared, "I can't believe I almost missed this. I was just walking back to the shelter when someone shouted, 'Candance, get in the van!' I didn't know where I was going, but I jumped in because I didn't want to be out in the cold. I can't believe I almost missed this. Thank you! This is one of the greatest nights of my life." Her words left me stunned. Was it really one of the greatest nights of her life? Once I gathered my thoughts, I replied, "Candance, it's our privilege to do this for you. We want you to know how much God truly loves you." She smiled and responded, "God must really love me tonight!"

We continued to dance, relishing the joy of the evening. Tragically, just a week later, I learned that Candance had been murdered. The news brought deep sorrow to our church community and served as a stark reminder of the importance of showing compassion to the poor and oppressed.

Candance's life was undoubtedly marked by hardships and daily struggles, and while I can only imagine the difficulties she faced, I take solace in knowing that, at least for one night, she experienced a glimpse of God's amazing love. Before her life was cut short, she had a chance to taste what it was like to be at God's banqueting table—a moment where a weak church, made up of imperfect people, created an experience that offered a taste of heaven here on earth.

The world is filled with people who struggle with hopelessness, and the most effective way to show compassion and love is by embracing our own weakness and brokenness first. It is through our vulnerabilities, much like how Jesus reached out to us, that we can truly become conduits of God's love and compassion to those in need.

Jesus had a remarkable ability to bring those on the fringes to the center, not through His impressive powers, but by connecting with them through His own vulnerability. This genuine connection is why so many of the greatest sinners of His time were drawn to Him. They were not captivated by His charisma alone but by the way He saw them and related to their weaknesses. When we minister from a place of weakness, we cannot judge others, for we understand what it feels like to hurt and be hopeless.

The Church is called to serve the poor and oppressed with profound compassion. Yet, the challenge remains: Will the church stand up and embrace its own weaknesses and truly serve in solidarity with the poor and oppressed? If we fail to do so, we risk causing more harm than good to those whom Jesus considers the least of these.

Notes

1. Luke 4:18–19.

2. Jim Wallis, *Who is My Neighbor?* (Washington, DC: Sojourners, 1994), 15.

3. Ron Sider, *Rich Christians in an Age of Hunger* (Dallas: Word Publishing, 1997), 49.

4. Isaiah 1:10–17.

5. Isaiah 58:3–7.

6. Jeremiah 22:13–19.

7. Matthew 25:31–46.

8. 1 John 3:17.

9. Sider, *Rich Christians in an Age of Hunger*, 16.

10. Richard Stern, *The Hole in Our Gospel* (Nashville: Thomas Nelson Publishing, 2009), 180.

11. Ibid., 185.

12. Sider, *Rich Christians in an Age of Hunger*, 50.

13. Stephen P. White, "Why We Need A Church That Is Poor And For The Poor," *Americamagazine.org*, September 08, 2015, accessed January 21, 2023, https://www.americamagazine.org/issue/213/they-know-suffering-christ?gclid=CjwKCAiA_6yfBhBNEiwAkmXy56QqlBhG-Sp1MmkRkyAkxYOOln_O032M5ZuFnMnd_6G98joBEcZq0xoCw_gQAvD_BwE/.

14. Ibid.

15. Sider, *Rich Christians in an Age of Hunger*, 50.

16. White, "Why We Need a Church that is Poor and for the Poor."

17. Jose L. Balado, *Mother Teresa In My Own Words* (New York: Random House Value Publishing, 1989), 28.

18. Mother Teresa, *The Love of Christ* (San Francisco: Harper and Row, 1982), 109.

19. Ibid., 114.

20. Wallis, *Who is My Neighbor?*, 16.

CHAPTER 9

Unwavering Commitment for Racial Justice

Racial justice is perhaps the most contentious issue within the church today. This profound division necessitates a dedicated chapter focusing on the racism that has infiltrated Christianity and how a Weak Church is uniquely equipped to pursue racial justice in a way that fosters true reconciliation and transformation. From its inception, the early Jerusalem Church, as depicted in Acts 15:1–35, resisted the inclusion of Gentiles into the Christian faith. The early Jewish Christians opposed the idea, insisting that faith in Jesus Christ remain an exclusively Jewish domain. They enforced this belief by demanding that Gentiles adhere to the laws of Moses and undergo circumcision. It was the Apostle Peter who had to intervene and dismantle these divisive requirements. His actions were a significant relief to Paul and Barnabas, who were advocating for a more inclusive faith. Peter's stance marked a crucial turning point, emphasizing that the message of Jesus was for all people, regardless of their ethnic background.

The Apostle Peter had come a long way. This was a far cry from his earlier days, when he was afraid to sit and eat with Gentile Christians for fear of judgment from his Jewish comrades. The Apostle Paul had to call him out on his hypocrisy in Galatians 2:11–14:

When Cephas came to Antioch, I opposed him to his face, because he stood condemned. For before certain men came from James, he used to eat with the Gentiles. But when they arrived, he began to draw back and separate himself from the Gentiles because he was afraid of those who belonged to the circumcision group. The other Jews joined him in his hypocrisy, so that by their hypocrisy even Barnabas was led astray. When I saw that they were not acting in line with the truth of the gospel, I said to Cephas in front of them all, "You are a Jew, yet you live like a Gentile and not like a Jew. How is it, then, that you force Gentiles to follow Jewish customs?

The Apostle Peter learned of his unconscious sin because the Apostle Paul had the courage to stand up and challenge his racist tendencies. Despite Peter's remarkable experiences, such as walking on water for a few seconds, using the power of the Holy Spirit to heal the sick, and spending three and a half years under the direct tutelage of Jesus Christ, he still needed guidance. Peter, with all his profound experiences and spiritual insights, required someone within the Body of Christ to teach him the true meaning of the Gospel and to confront him on how he was being complicit in racial injustice. Paul's boldness in addressing Peter's shortcomings was instrumental in helping him understand and embrace the inclusive nature of the Gospel message, demonstrating that even the most revered leaders are not beyond the need for correction and growth.

Over 2,000 years later, the church continues to be a divided house of worship. Nothing rings truer than the words of Martin Luther King Jr. when he boldly proclaimed on "Meet the Press" on April 17, 1960, that "11 o'clock on Sunday morning is one of the most segregated hours, if not the most segregated hour, in Christian America."[1] Sixty-five years later, Martin Luther King Jr.'s words still echo loudly through the walls of the American church. The Church remains one of the greatest, if not the greatest, institutions perpetuating racism.

But why? Why is the Church still so divided? I believe it is because of the Church's silence in addressing racial injustice. The topic of racism is exhausting and painful. It is not easy, and as Christians, we often gravitate toward what is easy.

There is a consensus among Christians that compassion-led ministries are a good area of focus for the Church. The act of serving and blessing people who are less fortunate than we are has always been accepted as a positive way to reflect God's love. Seldom will you hear Christian's debate about the importance of charity. In stark contrast, however, there is deep resistance when the focus shifts to "racial justice," despite it being a crucial aspect of equity rooted in the life, death, and resurrection of Jesus Christ.

There is a significant difference between compassion and justice. While Christian charity emphasizes the importance of serving the poor and oppressed, justice involves a different kind of work. For justice to be truly present among Christians and within the Church, God's people must first examine their own roles in perpetuating injustice.

This is why many churches and Christians hesitate to engage in justice work: the focus must shift inward rather than outward. We must ask ourselves, "How have I contributed to racial injustice?" Admitting personal complicity in racism is challenging, as it often connects to deep-seated generational sins. This requires us to explore how our families may have taught us to be segregated, despite our love for Jesus.

Confronting this reality is difficult and painful, but it is essential for embracing the full Gospel, which includes a strong message of racial justice. This is exemplified by the Apostle Paul's confrontation of Peter. Peter, the Rock, despite being a foundational figure in the early Church, had to recognize and address his own complicity in racial bias against Gentiles. His growth as a Christian enabled him to become more inclusive of Gentile believers, as reflected in Acts 15:1–35.

A Weak Church will often attract people from different ethnic backgrounds—not through strategic planning or targeted outreach, but organically, through the shared experience of brokenness and struggle. Pain, hardships, and human frailty do not discriminate; they transcend race, culture, and class. In a Weak Church, people are drawn together not because they look alike, speak the same language, or share the same customs, but because they recognize their own struggles and limitations. When a church embraces its weakness, it becomes a welcoming space for people from all walks of life who long for authenticity and belonging.

However, it would be a serious mistake for a Weak Church to stop at merely celebrating the diversity in its community. While diversity is a beautiful expression of God's kingdom and should be acknowledged with joy, true unity requires more than representation—it demands the hard work of reconciliation.

A Weak Church must go further by addressing the racial biases, prejudices, and wounds that exist among different ethnic groups. Every culture carries its own history of biases, and many individuals have experienced pain—sometimes even from those within the very church they now call home. If these issues go unspoken, the church may appear diverse on the surface, but the community will remain shallow and disconnected, lacking the depth of true solidarity.

Because a Weak Church embraces vulnerability, it is uniquely positioned to facilitate honest and difficult conversations that lead to deeper understanding, trust, and restoration. Instead of avoiding the tensions that come with diversity, a Weak Church leans into them, fostering a community where people can wrestle with their own brokenness and confront the pain that divides us. This is where true unity is formed—not through forced diversity, but through a church that chooses to confront its struggles together, recognizing that weakness is not a barrier to love but the very foundation of it.

Coming Face to Face with the Korean Beast of Racism

My family hails from the Korean peninsula, with my father being North Korean and my mother South Korean. Growing up, my parents recounted the atrocities committed by the Japanese during their occupation of Korea from August 22, 1910, to August 15, 1945. They spoke of the inhumane violence inflicted upon Korean men, women, and children, including the forced sexual slavery of women and girls, known as "comfort women." However, my parents didn't share these stories with their children merely as historical facts; they used them to instill a deep-seated animosity toward the Japanese, teaching my sisters and me to view them as inherently evil for their actions. Instead of focusing on the universal truth that all humans are born with a sinful nature, my parents framed the Japanese as the embodiment of evil. This belief colored my view for many years.

Similarly, my parents fostered negative views toward Black and Brown people in the United States. They owned a business on Broadway in the Upper West Side of New York City, where most of their customers were from these communities. While theft and other incidents are common in retail, an especially traumatic event occurred when my parents were held at gunpoint and beaten by four men—two Black and two Latino. The theft and violence led to the closure of our jewelry store.

In the Korean vernacular, the term for Black people translates to "dirt," an overtly racist expression that perpetuates the belief in the inferiority of Black individuals compared to Koreans. This derogatory term reinforces the harmful stereotype that Black and Brown people are more prone to poverty, criminal behavior, and violence. Such prejudices were not confined to my parents but were widespread among many Korean Americans, particularly those who, like us, operated businesses in predominantly Black and Brown neighborhoods or lived in lower-income urban areas after immigrating to the United States.

Growing up in Northern New Jersey, I had little interaction with Black, Brown, or Japanese communities. However, my perspective began to change when I qualified for the Equal Opportunity Fund (EOF) in college, which provided financial assistance for my tuition. As part of the EOF program, I had to attend a six-week summer session on campus before my first semester. I was excited for the opportunity to get a head start but was taken aback when I realized that most of the EOF students were Black and Brown. This was a cultural shock for me, as I had not prepared for such a diverse environment.

When I met my roommate, Blake, who was Black, my mother was visibly concerned. She offered to drive me home if I wanted to leave, but I declined, even though I secretly wished I could go home. That first night, I couldn't sleep, fearing that Blake might harm me. This fear stemmed from the racist beliefs I had grown up with. However, as days passed, I got to know Blake and his friends. We bonded over basketball and billiard games and meals in the cafeteria. My time with them was eye-opening and transformative, challenging the harmful stereotypes I had been taught.

In my junior year, my roommate was a Japanese international student named Kenji. Kenji and his friends were fun, kind, and respectful, making him the best roommate I had ever had. We shared our dreams for after college, talked about the kind of woman we wanted to marry, and found common ground in our daily routines. Since I was an early riser and needed to go to bed by 11 p.m., Kenji agreed to adjust his sleep schedule if I watched Japanese news with him at dawn. We particularly enjoyed the sports highlights of his favorite baseball team, the Tigers, which aired early in the morning at 6 a.m. Sometimes, we even watched the games together when they were broadcasted.

My college experience was transformational in many ways—not just academically, but also personally. It forced me to confront and reevaluate the deep-seated racism I had internalized. Without the opportunity to room with Blake and Kenji, I might never have challenged the racial narratives ingrained in me.

Today, two of my soul mates are Black. I would do anything for these brothers of mine. We have entered each other's worlds, sharing our lives, experiences, and cultural backgrounds. My children call them "uncle," and their children do the same for me. Through countless conversations and shared experiences, we have taught and challenged each other about our respective cultures. This mutual exchange has allowed us to grow in our understanding and appreciation of one another. Through this journey, we have learned not only to love each other but also to deeply support and love each other's tribe.

I am deeply grateful for the handful of close relationships I share with Japanese pastors across the country. Despite our peoples' historically separate lives, we are intentionally creating opportunities to connect and share our experiences. By breaking down barriers and fostering unity, we demonstrate that true community knows no cultural bounds. The friendships we are forming are not merely symbolic; they are built on genuine mutual respect and shared faith, paving the way for a more inclusive and harmonious future for the next generation of Korean and Japanese pastors.

I am blessed to pastor a multi-racial church where God has literally brought the nations to us. This incredible diversity has given our congregation the opportunity to build bridges with over twenty-five different ethnic groups. It is a beautiful thing to witness Korean Americans developing friendships with Japanese Americans, Chinese Americans, Black Americans, Latin Americans, and White Americans in our congregation—something our parents' generation could never have imagined.

Building this type of community was challenging and often painful. Many hard conversations were necessary, feelings were hurt, and numerous sermons addressed our own complicity in racism. Tears were shed as we collectively took an internal look at ourselves and unpacked our role in perpetuating racial biases. We were only able to accomplish this because we are a church that finds its commonality in our weaknesses. Without this posture of vulnerability and self-reflection, we would not be the multi-racial church we are today.

It is essential for Christians to examine how our families may have perpetuated racial narratives that have made us complicit in racial injustice. This reflection is necessary for every believer, as failing to address it hinders our ability to fulfill the Great Commandment: to love God and love our neighbor.

Jesus teaches us this profound lesson through the Parable of the Good Samaritan, shared in Luke 10:25–37. An expert in the law, a man who diligently followed Moses' commandments, seeks validation from Jesus about his faithfulness. However, Jesus presents him with a story that challenges his understanding of who a neighbor is.

In the parable, a man traveling from Jerusalem is attacked and left for dead on the side of the road. Both a priest and a Levite, experts in Jewish law, see the wounded man but avoid him, fearing ritual impurity from the man's blood. Despite their adherence to the law, their actions lack compassion and disobedience.

Then, a Samaritan—despised by Jews for being a mixed race and considered heretical—stops to help. Samaritans, who were part Jewish and part Gentile, were deeply disliked by the Israelites. Yet this Samaritan not only tends to the man's wounds but also transports him to an inn, cares for him overnight, and ensures his continued care by promising to cover any additional expenses to the innkeeper.

Jesus asks the law expert which of the three was a true neighbor to the injured man. The expert responds, "The one who had mercy on him." Jesus then instructs, "Go and do likewise."[2]

Through this parable, Jesus teaches that our neighbor is often someone from a different ethnic background or even someone we might consider an enemy. We are called to love those we find difficult to love, those we might have been taught to distance ourselves from. Failing to love these individuals means failing to love God Himself. Consider who your neighbors are. Are they solely people you get along with and who share the same ethnic background? The Jewish people in the first century believed this. Jesus teaches us that such thinking is failing to live out the Great Commandment. Reflect on those you have distanced yourself from or deemed unforgivable. Jesus calls us to love them.

This is the heart of the Gospel: our love for God is intimately linked to our love for our enemies. The Apostle Paul emphasized this critical element of the Gospel to the church in Ephesus, highlighting its enduring relevance. The Gospel is not just about our reconciliation with God through Jesus Christ's death and resurrection but also about dismantling the walls of racial hostility that separate us. Reflect on Paul's powerful message in Ephesians 2:1–22:

> As for you, you were dead in your transgressions and sins, in which you used to live when you followed the ways of this world and of the ruler of the kingdom of the air, the spirit who is now at work in those who are disobedient. All of us also lived among them at one time, gratifying the cravings of our flesh and following its desires and thoughts. Like the rest, we were by nature deserving of wrath. But because of his great love for us, God, who is rich in mercy, made us alive with Christ even when we were dead in transgressions—it is by grace you have been saved. And God raised us up with Christ and seated us with him in the heavenly realms in Christ Jesus, in order that in the coming ages he might show the incomparable riches of his grace, expressed in his kindness to us in Christ Jesus. For it is by grace you have been saved, through faith—and this is not from yourselves, it is the gift of God—not by works, so that no one can boast. For we are God's handiwork, created in Christ Jesus to do good works, which God prepared in advance for us to do. Therefore, remember that formerly you who are Gentiles by birth and called "uncircumcised" by those who call themselves "the circumcision" (which is done in the body by human hands)—remember that at that time you were separate from Christ, excluded from citizenship in Israel and foreigners to the covenants of the promise, without hope and without God in the world. But now in Christ Jesus you who once were far away have been brought near by the blood of Christ. For he himself is our peace, who has made the two groups one and has destroyed the barrier, the dividing wall of hostility, by setting aside in his flesh the law with its commands and regulations. His purpose was to create in himself one new humanity out of the two, thus making peace, and in one body to reconcile both of them to God through the cross, by which he put to death their hostility. He came and preached peace to you who were far away and peace to those who were near. For through him we both have access to the Father by one Spirit.

> Consequently, you are no longer foreigners and strangers, but fellow citizens with God's people and also members of his household, built on the foundation of the apostles and prophets, with Christ Jesus himself as the chief cornerstone. In him the whole building is joined together and rises to become a holy temple in the Lord. And in him you too are being built together to become a dwelling in which God lives by his Spirit.

The heart of the Gospel message extends beyond our reconciliation with God; it also encompasses racial reconciliation with those we might consider our enemies. This profound truth, eloquently taught by Paul, has been overlooked by many churches for over 2,000 years. The essence of evangelism is not just leading people to faith in Jesus Christ, but demonstrating that our faith can achieve what the world cannot: loving our enemies. Our faith has the power to unite Jews and Gentiles, men and women, slaves and free people in a deep and meaningful unity through Jesus Christ. As Galatians 3:28 states, "There is neither Jew nor Gentile, neither slave nor free, nor is there male and female, for you are all one in Christ Jesus."

At a CCDA conference I attended several years ago, the late Richard Twiss, a Native American educator and author, shared an unforgettable insight about the beauty and necessity of racial diversity and the Trinity. He said, "In order for there to be unity, there must first be diversity. God is One because He is Three."

There is a wealth of literature on racial justice, yet I haven't encountered any that emphasize the importance of approaching this issue by coming to the table with our weaknesses. I believe that for the Church to make meaningful progress toward racial justice, our shared commonality must be our weaknesses. By focusing on our shared weaknesses, we create a foundation for constructive, honest conversations about race, rather than falling into defensiveness or blame.

While we must celebrate the rich diversity that exists in our world as a reflection of God's Kingdom, we cannot overlook the dark, demonic forces that seek to divide rather than unite us. This tragic reality is rooted in the pervasive nature of sin, which has woven itself into the fabric of our everyday lives. One of the most insidious manifestations of this dark power is how it has divided humanity along racial lines, constructing false hierarchies of dominance and oppression.

In the history of the United States, we have witnessed this system of domination being perpetuated primarily by White people, who have historically held positions of power. The idea of Whiteness, when weaponized, serves to undermine the biblical truth that all races are equally created in the image of

God. This oppressive framework seeks to distort God's design for humanity, turning diversity—a gift from God—into a tool for division and subjugation.

The weight of this history, marked by slavery, segregation, and systemic discrimination, has left deep scars on the fabric of American society. And, unfortunately, the echoes of this domination continue to resonate today, as systems and attitudes rooted in this racial hierarchy persist. The demonic power behind these divisions is not merely a historical footnote; it continues to actively pit people against each other, elevating the White race while relegating all other ethnicities to positions of subordination.

The challenge for every ethnic group today is to recognize that we are all contending against this spiritual and societal force—a power that seeks to distort God's vision of unity by placing one race above all others. It is a spiritual battle, not just a sociological one. As believers, we are called to confront this darkness head-on, proclaiming the truth that every person, regardless of race, is fearfully and wonderfully made in the image of God. We must resist the temptation to perpetuate these divisions and instead strive to embody the unity and love that Christ calls us to in His Kingdom.

Here are some personal challenges that are particularly relevant to specific ethnic groups. Throughout my years of pastoring a multi-racial church and building deep, meaningful friendships with individuals from White, Asian, Black, and Latin communities, I have gained a wealth of insights and perspectives. These experiences have shaped my understanding of both the beauty and challenges that come with living out the Gospel in a diverse and complex world. My hope is that these reflections will serve to both encourage and challenge the body of Christ as a whole—pushing us to grow in our love for one another and in our commitment to justice, unity, and reconciliation. I present these challenges to you with the hope that they resonate, especially if you identify with the ethnic group mentioned. It's important to recognize and address these issues, as they can deeply impact our experiences and interactions within our community. Please remember, read this from a place where you have embraced your weakness. I am writing this from that perspective and hope that in our shared weakness, God's strength will be perfected in us.

White Americans

One of the most difficult truths for White Christians to face is the substantial historical role that their communities and churches have played in perpetuating racial injustice. It can be particularly difficult for White Americans, especially Christians, to fully grasp the depth of the racialized system in which they live. Immersed in a society that has long upheld structures of

White power, it becomes challenging to discern the ways in which these systems subtly shape their worldview, privileges, and even their understanding of faith. The task before White Christians is not a simple one; it calls for deep introspection and a willingness to confront uncomfortable truths about their place within this hierarchy.

The challenge posed to White Christians is monumental: Will they embrace the full scope of the Gospel, with all of its implications for justice, equality, and reconciliation? This means more than just personal transformation; it requires a bold, public stand against the pervasive power of Whiteness that has historically, and continues to, oppress others. Will they have the courage to renounce systems of domination and choose the path of sacrificial love, standing alongside brothers and sisters of all races to dismantle structures that perpetuate inequality?

Daniel Hill, in his book *White Lies*, exposes the truth of racial systems that divide the Church. He gives practical insights on how the Church can resist these racial systems. The Church is the greatest force that has sustained racism in our country. Hill, along with Dr. William Jennings, contends that White Supremacy is a parasite. For a parasite to thrive, it needs a host. Daniel Hill and Dr. Jennings both make the thundering claim that the host of White Supremacy is Christianity.[3] "One of the greatest threats facing American Christianity is the severe divide along racial lines that continue to grow more severe with each passing year. The 2016 and 2020 elections served to bring the divide to the forefront."[4]

Churches in America—and White churches in particular—are the greatest institutions that feed the power of racism in our society. This is a scary truth that must be acknowledged and dealt with in our churches. Swanson exposes the truth that "White evangelical Protestants support political movements to ban or severely restrict refugees at rates higher than almost every other demographic. More than any other religious group, White evangelicals believe that increasing cultural diversity in the United States is a negative development."[5]

The sad result of this pattern is that Christianity in the United States continues to be dominated by White evangelicalism. While this may be a difficult truth to swallow, it is certainly not a difficult one to see. Just take a moment to consider the songs we sing during worship at church or the authors we have come to acknowledge as authorities on spiritual matters. Who are the leading voices that are heard in most of the mega-conferences offered in America or even around the world? As we take a closer look at Christianity today, it becomes evident that a significant majority of the people who make up mainstream "Christendom" are White evangelicals.

In his book *White Lies*, Daniel Hill exposes the self-deception that allows many, particularly White people, to ignore racism in our country. He argues that White culture is a powerful force that often dominates other cultures. As a result, White Culture is a powerful force that often destroys anything in its path. He says, "When White culture comes in contact with other cultures, it almost always wins . . . the system of race in America has consistently treated White people as a superior race and has consistently treated non-Whites as inferior."[6]

Bryan Stevenson, who is the founder of *Equal Justice Initiative*, calls the racial inequities in America a result of "the narrative of racial difference." He says in an interview:

> You can't understand many of the most destructive issues or policies in our country without understanding our history of racial inequality. And I actually think it begins with our interaction with native people because we took land, we killed people, we disrupted a culture. We were brutal. And we justified and rationalized that land grab, that genocide, by characterizing native people as different. It was the first way in which this narrative of racial difference was employed to justify behaviors that would otherwise be unjustifiable. When you are allowed to demonize another community and call them savages, and treat them brutally and cruelly, it changes your psyche. We abused and mistreated the communities and cultures that existed on this land before Europeans arrived, and then that narrative of racial difference was used to develop slavery. . . . I genuinely believe that, despite all of that victimization, the worst part of slavery was this narrative that we created about black people—this idea that black people aren't fully human, that they are three-fifths human, that they are not capable, that they are not evolved. That ideology, which set up white supremacy in America, was the most poisonous and destructive consequence of two centuries of slavery. And I do believe that we never addressed it.[7]

In a Strong Church, especially in a Strong White Church, racial justice is seldom addressed. The nomenclature that is often used to justify this omission is that racial justice is "too political and not Biblical." As a result, the Strong Church will always direct its outreach endeavors toward compassion-type ministries. David Swanson, a pastor and author, shares that "it can be painful to acknowledge how inept White Christianity has been at confronting the destructive narrative of racial difference and the racial practices that shape our habits."[8] Jemar Tisby, author of *Color of Compromise*, says in an interview with *Christianity Today*, "Many churches are either unaware or unwilling to acknowledge publicly the role which race has played in their founding or in the ongoing practices or policies of the church. These things simply need to be excavated in most cases. Only then can you go about the relational work, asking what reconciliation means in light of a particular church's past."[9] The Kingdom of God, which Christians have been charged to advance by our very King, Jesus Christ, will continue to be compromised if racial justice is not addressed and taught as part of the Gospel message in churches, especially in White churches.

In a Weak Church, passion for racial justice is deeply embedded into its ethos. As mentioned before, the most effective way a church can embrace and champion racial justice is through vulnerability. Racial justice cannot flourish when we are leaning on our strengths. Strength-focused work of this kind will often lead to finger-pointing of others or complete disregard of the pains of our fellow brothers and sisters. Our weaknesses disarm our strengths and create a safe place for us to empathize and learn, which in turn will motivate us to stand alongside those who are being oppressed because of the color of their skin. Dr. Brenda Salter McNeil, professor and author of racial justice, calls this process "identification"—where "your people" become "my people."

> The identification phase is about working together with the people in this particular group to change the way you interact with one another. The ways that people interact, or ways that they should interact, usually need to be renegotiated in order for true reconciliation to come about. In other words, the ethos of the group as a whole undergoes transformation during the identification portion of the journey. Automatic perceptions and stereotypes will need to be confronted and worked through, empathy needs room to grow, and mutual understanding must have space to develop.[10]

Racism has been a core tenet of this country from its very inception. For the past 245 years, racism in this country has manifested as genocides, slavery, and other horrific events. It has created a social structure in which White people remain at the top of the social ladder. The Church has not only been complicit, but more tragically, has served as the host on which the parasite of racism has fed and thrived.

Will White Christians and their churches confront this uncomfortable truth, not only by discussing it but also by incorporating it into their Christian discipleship? David Swanson tackles this issue in his book, *Rediscipling the White Church*. He calls on White churches to revamp their discipleship model to prioritize racial justice. Swanson recognizes the challenges White churches face in shifting their discipleship focus toward racial justice, because "White Christianity is deeply susceptible to and complicit in the racial biases that inflict damage on people of color."[11]

To White pastors leading multi-ethnic churches, I commend your commitment to racial justice. However, I'd like to urge you to think about potentially leaving your multi-ethnic churches and pastoring a predominately White congregation. White Evangelical Christians will not recognize their complicity in racism unless someone from within their community not only calls them out but also pastors them through the process.

Could this be your Nineveh that you might be avoiding? I understand the sacrifice is significant, and like Jonah, you may resist and even try to flee. Nevertheless, I encourage you to seek God's direction in this matter. If more "woke" White pastors are willing to make this sacrifice and endure the challenges of pastoring a White church, we might witness something beautiful—the potential eradication of racism.

Movements are born when Christian leaders are willing to rise up, make sacrifices, and stand against their own community to expose sin. By doing so, we can hope for a transformative change.

Asian Americans

There are forty-eight distinct Asian ethnic groups, and while I can't address all of them, I'll focus primarily on the Korean American diaspora. As Koreans, it's crucial to recognize that our aspiration has often been to emulate White Americans. We aimed to achieve the same success and wealth, which is why our parents placed such a strong emphasis on education and demanded exceptional grades. This desire to mirror White Americans extends beyond financial success; it also includes physical appearance, as evidenced by the prevalence of plastic surgery among Koreans to enhance White features like the eyes, nose, and other facial traits.

The fact is that Asians have achieved notable success. Asian Americans are now the wealthiest ethnic group in the United States, surpassing White Americans in net worth, according to Pew Research. "In 2021, Asian households had a median net worth of $320,900, compared with $250,400 for White households. The median net worth of Hispanic households ($48,700) and Black households ($27,100) was much less."[12]

However, this financial success, particularly among Korean Americans, can create the illusion that we are on equal footing with White Americans or, at the very least, on the same team. This misconception can foster a sense of pride and superiority over Black and Latin Americans, bolstered by impressive numbers. Despite this, we must remember that, regardless of our financial status, we remain ethnic minorities in this country. Asians can never benefit from White privilege. No matter how much we may desire it, that privilege will never truly be ours. Although we may live in nice houses and drive fancy cars, we do not share the same power and privilege as White

Americans. Unfortunately, many Asian Americans have aligned themselves with White Americans and adopted similar views toward Black, Latin, and Native Americans, forgetting that economic success does not equate to social power or equality.

Viet Thanh Nguyen, a Pulitzer Prize–winning author, boldly claims that:

> Asian Americans are caught between the perception that we are inevitably foreign and the temptation that we can be allied with white people in a country built on white supremacy. As a result, anti-Black (and anti-brown and anti-Native) racism runs deep in Asian-American communities. . . . Throughout Asian-American history, Asian immigrants and their descendants have been offered the opportunity by both Black people and white people to choose sides in the Black-white racial divide, and we have far too often chosen the white side. Asian Americans, while actively critical of anti-Asian racism, have not always stood up against anti-Black racism. Frequently, we have gone along with the status quo and affiliated with white people.[13]

Could this be why Asians feel unsettled and upset when they hear about the Black Lives Matter rallies? Have Asians chosen to align with White Americans and fear damaging that relationship? Is this why some Asian American Christians view supporting the civil rights of Black and Brown people as political rather than biblical, even though we've established that racial justice is a core part of the Gospel message?

Could supporting the rights of Black and Brown people make Asians feel like they are choosing the other side, placing us in the Black and Brown diaspora and obligating us to share their burdens—burdens we've strived to avoid? Could it be that supporting these communities would make White Americans see us differently, no longer viewing us as the "model minority," and instead treating us like they treat Black, Brown, and Native communities?

Another aspect to consider is the history of wounds: many Asian immigrants were often verbally and physically assaulted by members of the Black and Brown communities when they moved into their neighborhoods. Could this be a reason we've aligned with White people?

These are critical questions to reflect and wrestle with, as they are seldom discussed in conversations about racial relationships involving Asian Americans.

Nguyen argues that the term "model minority," a label given to Asians by White Americans, is problematic; he argues that it means "to be invisible in most circumstances because we are doing what we are supposed to be doing, like my parents, until we become hypervisible because we are doing what we do too well, like the Korean shopkeepers. Then the model minority becomes the Asian invasion."[14]

As Asian Americans, we need to confront the harsh reality that the White community has committed a grave injustice on our people. We may have been led to believe that we stand alongside the White community, yet, in doing so, we may have unknowingly absorbed a mindset that discourages us from fully embracing our Black and Brown brothers and sisters in Christ. It's time to acknowledge this distortion and reclaim the call to love and stand in solidarity with all members of God's family.

For Asian pastors and church leaders of predominantly Asian congregations, it is crucial to address this issue with your congregation. We need to recognize our complicity in racism against the Black and Brown communities. Educating our church community on this matter is imperative and a discipleship issue, as supporting the Black and Brown communities is not about choosing sides, but about loving our neighbors as ourselves.

Furthermore, as Asian Americans, we must sincerely repent and seek forgiveness from the Black and Brown communities for aligning ourselves with the White community and being complicit in racial injustice. This affiliation has often led us to overlook and, at times, perpetuate the systemic racism that oppresses our Black and Brown brothers and sisters. Our repentance must be heartfelt and accompanied by meaningful actions.

In addition to that, Asians must be grateful to and honor the Black community. Their courageous fight and sacrifices for the civil rights for all peoples have allowed Asian Americans to prosper in the United States. While we have indeed worked hard as a community, it is essential to acknowledge that without the establishment of the Civil Rights Acts on July 2, 1964, we would not be where we are today as an ethnic group.

I wonder what it would look like if the Asian, Black, and Brown communities stood united to combat racial injustice in the United States. While my faith in the country achieving this unity is limited, my hope for the church is strong. By embracing our weaknesses and humbling ourselves, I believe we can fully embrace the Gospel and learn to love both God and our neighbors as ourselves.

Black and Brown Americans

I don't intend to lump Black and Brown (Latino) Americans together intentionally. I recognize the significant differences between the Black and Latino communities. The only reason why they are under the same heading here is because I know very little about what it feels like to be Black or Brown in the United States. I can never walk a mile in your shoes, nor do I claim to be an expert in your experiences. This will be brief, but I hope it is both challenging and helpful.

Have you considered how difficult it is to give up power? Those who possess it rarely want to relinquish it, even when it's the right thing to do. This resistance is part of our sinful nature. When someone has power, surrendering it becomes incredibly challenging. This is why the incarnation of Jesus Christ is so extraordinary. Jesus, who was God, had all the power in the universe. Yet, He chose to surrender that power and humbly become a weak, powerless human being. Only God can do something like this with ease; but for us humans, giving up power is incredibly difficult.

Those without power may think it's easy to give it up. However, we must recognize how hard it is for White Americans to surrender the power and privilege they've built over the centuries. Yes, change is necessary, but we shouldn't simply expect the White community to relinquish power easily.

If White Christians and their churches are willing to embrace their weaknesses and surrender their power, shouldn't we give them time and space to grieve? This may sound controversial or even heretical to some, but any loss requires a time of grieving for strong mental health. Perhaps White people hold onto White privilege not because they believe it's right or love the idea, but because they're fearful of what life will be like without it. As minorities, we may understand this, but for the majority, the fear of losing power and control is significant and many times terrifying.

Instead of assuming this will be easy for White Americans, let's empathize with how difficult it will be for them. This empathy might encourage White Christians and assure them that sacrificing their power is well worth the effort.

Lastly, to the Black and Brown communities, I ask you to consider the wounds inflicted on the Asian community, particularly those of us who lived in the same cities or towns where some of you may have grown up. Speaking on behalf of the Korean American community, I ask: Why were we often bullied in our neighborhoods and schools for being Korean? We assume that you understand the pain of being recipients of racism, so why direct such prejudice toward Koreans and other Asian communities?

We acknowledge that sin often perpetuates more sin, and that many of these actions may be rooted in deeper systemic issues. However, it's important to recognize that a significant number of Asians still carry feelings of anger and bitterness toward Black and Brown communities as a result of these racial injustices. Many Asian Americans who immigrated to the United States between the 1960s and 1990s faced hardship, discrimination, and sometimes direct hostility from Black and Brown individuals while striving to build a better life for their families. These experiences have left lasting wounds, complicating the dynamics between these communities and highlighting the complex nature of racial tension in America.

Acknowledging this shared pain can be a powerful step toward healing and reconciliation. It can help bridge the divide between the Asian, Black, and Brown communities and foster a deeper understanding and mutual respect. Together, we can work toward creating a more inclusive and supportive environment for all marginalized groups, ensuring that no one has to suffer the pain of racism and discrimination.

The Nuts and Bolts of Racial Justice at Metro Community Church

Addressing racial justice has been one of the most significant challenges for Metro Community Church. I wish I could say it was easy, but it has consistently been a struggle for our weak church.

Years ago, the elders and I recognized that to truly integrate justice, advocacy, and compassion into our ethos, we needed dedicated leadership. Without a focused effort, we risked being more talk than action. So, we made the decision to hire a full-time staff member to oversee our Justice, Advocacy, and Compassion (JAC) Ministry. This ministry is not a sub-ministry; it is the heart and soul of our church.

Though it took time and considerable effort, with the leadership of our JAC pastor and Elder Board, we made significant progress. It hasn't been without its growing pains and challenges, but together, we've worked through these difficulties.

Here's a list of some of the initiatives we've undertaken and continue to pursue at Metro to uphold our unwavering commitment to racial justice:

- Preach regarding racial justice regularly on Sundays.
- Establish a racially diverse elder board.
- Establish a racially diverse staff.
- Create a Cultural Immersion Small Group—watch Black, Latino, and Asian films and documentaries and discuss together.
- Offer Dinners for Eight—eight people from the church gather at someone's house for dinner and share about their experiences with racism.
- Sing worship songs that are not exclusively CCM, but also intentionally incorporate other genres of worship music such as gospel, Latin, and Asian song writers.

- Celebrate an Annual Cultural Day—twenty-five distinct culture groups within the church are represented as they come together and celebrate their culture with food and arts.
- Celebrate Black, Asian, and Latin History months on Sundays.
- Establish a Racial Righteousness Team that allows sacred spaces for our Black, Brown, and Asian communities to lament and learn from the racial injustice in our country.
- Offer an eight-week Asian American History Workshops.
- Offer a twelve-week Black History Workshop.
- Organize Black Lives Matter and Stop Asian Hate Marches.
- Participate and celebrate Martin Luther King Jr. Day with Black congregations in our neighborhood.
- Establish the Korean and Black Pastors Association to unite Black and Korean churches in building a stronger, more connected community.
- Organize joint worship services with Black congregations in our town and county.

At Metro Community Church, full support of our commitment to racial justice is a requirement for membership in the church. Given the polarizing and complex nature of racial justice, it's crucial for individuals to be unwavering in their commitment. Without this dedication, they may find themselves leaving the church when faced with discomfort or disagreements—a pattern that has occurred throughout our church's history.

Seventy percent of Metro Community Church is Asian American, with Korean Americans being the largest ethnic group. We are also 15 percent Black, 10 percent Latino, and 5 percent White. For eighteen of our twenty-one years, we have intentionally been located in a predominantly Black and Latino section of Englewood. As a result, we have become an incarnational presence in our city, and our diverse community—comprising Asian, Black, Brown, and White members—is learning to embrace one another as brothers and sisters in Christ. This has required significant sacrifice, hard work, and an unwavering commitment to racial justice, even in the face of people leaving the church.

On February 26, 2012, Trayvon Martin was tragically shot and killed. In the weeks that followed, I learned that several of our Black staff, elders, and congregation members had attended Black churches to mourn another senseless loss in a pattern all too familiar. When I asked some of our Black leaders why they chose to lament elsewhere, they told me, "Peter, we love Metro, but we don't feel it's a place where Black people can mourn and seek justice when we are being killed without cause." Their honesty was a wake-up call for me, and I deeply appreciated their vulnerability.

I called a meeting with my Executive Pastor, the Director of JAC, the Spiritual Formation Pastor, and some Black leaders from our church. It was clear to me that we were failing in this area, and I took responsibility for it. Our Black leaders expressed a strong need for Metro to address racial disparities and inequities, particularly regarding law enforcement, from the pulpit. For Metro to be a church that truly sees each other as brothers and sisters in Christ and ministers from a place of genuine weakness, we needed to grow in our empathy for the struggles of our Black and Brown community. They felt we were falling short, and it became clear that addressing these issues from the pulpit needed to be a regular part of our preaching, not just a one-time event.

When I began to address racial justice regularly from the pulpit, some members of our Asian and White community were upset. I received emails accusing me of preaching heresy and committing a grave sin. Many insisted that racism no longer existed in America, citing the presence of a Black president as proof. This backlash led to about fifty people leaving the church, including several leaders I had personally mentored and counseled. Their departure along with the loss of their financial contributions—approximately $250,000—placed Metro in a severe financial crisis. For the first time, I had to consider laying off staff members. I was heartbroken and felt like a failure.

I faced a major challenge: Should I cease preaching and take a bold stance on racial justice to halt the exodus, or should I continue to preach and teach that racial justice is a fundamental part of the Gospel and the Great Commandment? I chose to remain steadfast in my commitment to the latter. I believed in this principle with every fiber of my being and was prepared to make this sacrifice, even if it meant that the majority of our church might leave.

Today, Metro Community Church is more vibrant and fuller of life than it was in 2012–2015. I've come to realize that the departure of those fifty people, though painful, was necessary for God to accomplish the work he intended through our church. While I would never want to go through such a trial again, the sacrifice was worth it. If faced with a similar situation, I would choose the same path once more.

A Weak Church is uniquely positioned to pursue racial justice because it acknowledges that weakness, brokenness, and humility are the very pathways to reconciliation. Rather than avoiding the discomfort of racial tensions, a Weak Church leans into them, recognizing that confronting injustice requires honesty, repentance, and a willingness to listen. Just as a Weak Church embraces vulnerability within its own community, it also stands in solidarity with the marginalized, refusing to turn a blind eye to oppression. In a world where power, privilege, and self-preservation often dictate the conversation, a Weak Church operates differently—it does not seek to dominate or defend, but to lament, learn, and love in the way of Jesus. Only by embracing our collective weakness can we dismantle the walls that divide us and move toward a justice that is not just spoken about, but lived out in radical, restorative ways.

Pastors and church leaders, what will you do? Will you take a stand? Will you fully embrace the Gospel and teach your congregation about the centrality of racial justice as part of the Gospel and the Great Commandment? If so, be prepared for the challenges and trials that may arise. I assure you, the experience will ultimately strengthen you.

Perhaps, in doing so, we can fulfill Jesus' last prayer: "My prayer is not for them alone. I pray also for those who will believe in me through their message, that all of them may be one, Father, just as you are in me and I am in you. May they also be in us so that the world may believe that you have sent me."[15]

It's time for the church to separate themselves from the culture so that Christ stands above it. Until the church is willing to make an unwavering commitment for racial justice, they have unconsciously chosen to have the culture stand above Christ.

Notes

1. "The Most Segregated Hour in America—Martin Luther King Jr," *YouTube*, uploaded by Jason Tripp, April 29, 2014, https://www.youtube.com/watch?v =1q881g1L_d8.

2. Luke 10:36–37.

3. Daniel Hill, *White Lies* (Grand Rapids: Zondervan Books, 2020), 2.

4. Ibid., 12.

5. David Swanson, *Rediscipling the White Church* (Downers Grove: Intervarsity Press, 2020), 20.

6. Daniel Hill, *White Awake* (Downers Grove: Intervarsity Press, 2017), 51–53.

7. James McWilliams, "Bryan Stevenson on What Well-Meaning White People Need to Know About Race," *Pacific Standard*, updated February 19, 2019, accessed January 21, 2023, https://psmag.com/magazine/bryan-stevenson-ps-interview.

8. Swanson, *Rediscipling the White Church*, 25.

9. Myles Wentz, "Jemar Tisby: Three Words Should Guide Our Pursuit Of Racial Justice," *Christianity Today*, June 10, 2021, accessed March 4, 2023, https://www .christianitytoday.com/ct/2021/june-web-only/jemar-tisby-how-fight-racism-three -words.html.

10. Brenda Salter McNeil, *Roadmap to Reconciliation 2.0* (Downers Grove: Inter-Varsity Press, 2020), 73.

11. Swanson, *Rediscipling the White Church*, 12.

12. Rakesh Kochhar and Mohamad Moslimani, "Wealth Gaps Across Racial and Ethnic Groups," *Pew Research*, December 2, 2023, accessed July 24, 2024, https://www.pewresearch.org/2023/12/04/wealth-gaps-across-racial-and-ethnicgroups/#:~:text=Asian%20households%20overall%20had%20more,(%2427%2C100)%20was%20much%20less.\.

13. Viet Thanh Nguyen, "Asian Americans Are Still Caught in the Trap of the 'Model Minority" Stereotype. And It Creates Inequality for All," *Time*, June 26, 2020, accessed July 24, 2024, https://time.com/5859206/anti-asian-racism-america/.

14. Ibid.

15. John 17:20–21.

CHAPTER 10

Creating and Maintaining a Vulnerable Church Staff Culture

A congregation cannot become a Weak Church unless its staff first learns to embrace and lead from a place of vulnerability. The staff plays a critical role in establishing the ethos and setting the pace at which the church community becomes a space where weakness is acknowledged and shared. Although incarnational preaching initiates this process and sets the tone for the depth of vulnerability the church will experience, it is the staff who are the foot soldiers that carry out the mission of weakness for the church. Moreover, they are responsible for cultivating environments where individuals feel safe to confront and embrace their own weaknesses. This dual responsibility—leading by example and creating safe, open spaces—ensures that vulnerability is not just preached but lived out within the life of the church.

The best place for staff to learn and embody this ethos is during weekly staff meetings. These meetings should become the space where the ethos of vulnerability is not only taught but practiced, equipping staff to then instill this culture within their own ministries as they have learned and experienced it in staff meetings.

In a Strong Church, staff meetings are often focused on business and tasks, leaving little room for personal sharing or vulnerability. Consequently, the church struggles to embrace its weaknesses because the staff does not set the tone for openness. Staff members in such environments rarely feel empowered or encouraged to discuss their struggles with colleagues. Many pastors and staff members even go so far as to hide their difficulties from those they work alongside, as the prevailing culture does not welcome or support expressions of weakness. This lack of openness contributes significantly to burnout, as the relentless pressure to perform is often the only experience staff members encounter. They frequently feel acknowledged by senior leaders only when they achieve high performance, leaving them to feel overlooked or invisible among their peers otherwise.

The challenges faced by staff members are not limited to their external responsibilities; the internal culture of the staff further compounds their struggles by failing to minister to them in meaningful ways. While the church staff is expected to minister to the congregation, the question arises: Who is responsible for ministering to them? Unfortunately, it is often not the senior leaders during staff meetings. As a result, these meetings are not something that staff members look forward to. Yet, staff meetings present a prime opportunity to minister to the needs of the staff, an opportunity that is frequently missed.

Building a healthy ethos among staff is crucial to the success of any organization. It's no surprise that there's a wealth of literature on how leaders can cultivate such an environment within their companies. Unfortunately, a search for guidance on creating a healthy ethos within a church yields results that focus almost exclusively on church growth. Because of this gap, I will primarily draw from business literature, where the concepts of ethos and culture have been explored with greater diversity and depth in the secular context.

An organization's ethos encompasses its character, culture, and shared values. It is the foundation that attracts the right people to the organization and is essential for fostering staff team chemistry, especially during challenging times. For instance, the COVID-19 pandemic posed a significant test to the ethos of many companies. Some employers now prefer their employees to work exclusively from home, which can be a loss for those who thrive in a collaborative, in-person environment. On the other hand, some employers are insisting that employees return to the office, leading to a wave of resignations from those who prefer remote work.

Jane Sparrow, writing for *Forbes*, emphasizes that in the post-pandemic era, leaders must prioritize their company's ethos. She argues that this should be a key focus for every leader. Sparrow asserts that building a healthy ethos requires leaders to establish genuine human connections with their teams. She writes that "Processes and policies are practical, functional things that are necessary, but they are limited in their usefulness when managing change. These tools will not take your people emotionally on the journey with you. Especially in times of flux, the leader must do more than manage; they must make a human connection, revisit the company ethos and refine if necessary, and sometimes win hearts and minds all over again."[1]

Pastors, when was the last time you truly connected with your staff on a human level? It's rare for me to hear colleagues in ministry who serve in multi-staff churches talk about having a genuine connection with their senior or executive pastor. The most common compliment I hear is that their senior or executive pastor is funny and makes staff meetings enjoyable. While fun and laughter are important, there also needs to be moments when senior leaders make meaningful connections with their staff. Genuine human connection requires senior leaders to exemplify vulnerability and create an environment of care and openness among the team.

I wonder what propelled Jesus to confide with His three closest disciples—Peter, James, and John—that His soul was overwhelmed to the point of death. In that moment, Jesus was revealing His deep sense of brokenness and weakness. The Scripture tells us, "Then Jesus went with His disciples to a place called Gethsemane, and He said to them, 'Sit here while I go over there and pray.' He took Peter and the two sons of Zebedee along with Him, and He began to be sorrowful and troubled. Then He said to them, 'My soul is overwhelmed with sorrow to the point of death. Stay here and keep watch with me.'"[2]

How was Jesus, their leader, able to be so vulnerable? Didn't He, like many of us in leadership roles, feel the immense pressure to hide His struggles from those He led? The weight of leadership often compels us to project strength and assurance, leaving little room to reveal our own weaknesses. Yet Jesus chose a different path. He didn't conceal His deep anguish and sorrow; instead, He openly shared it with His closest disciples. This transparency wasn't a sign of weakness but a testament to His unmatched character and integrity.

Jesus understood that true leadership isn't about maintaining a façade of invulnerability. It's about being real, honest, and human. By sharing His sorrow, He demonstrated that even the strongest leaders need support and understanding. This act of vulnerability didn't diminish His authority or respect among His disciples. On the contrary, it deepened their connection, forging a bond of trust and empathy that was unparalleled.

His openness allowed Peter, James, and John to see the depth of His humanity, which only strengthened their loyalty and love for Him. They were not just followers; they became His confidants, entrusted with the raw and unfiltered reality of His suffering. This kind of connection is rare, especially in leadership, but it's what set Jesus apart. His willingness to be vulnerable not only showcased His integrity but also created a model of leadership rooted in authenticity and deep, personal connection.

Erick Iverson, a writer for Fast Company, argues that ethos cannot be cultured through a set of core values and an employee handbook. Ethos is what gives organizations their unique character. Iverson goes as far as to say that a strong ethos in a company "help attract and retain top talent, foster innovation, and build a sense of shared purpose and pride. It can also lead to better decision-making, greater customer satisfaction, and improved financial results."[3] A healthy culture is a result of the shared values, beliefs, and behaviors that everyone in an organization has and continues to contribute to. Iverson believes that each employee in a company has the power to shape the culture. Iverson says nothing will destroy a culture faster than "disingenuous leadership." He writes that "it's one thing to have individuals who don't align with the corporate culture. It's a much more challenging scenario when you are told that you are a culture fit, but you see your leadership making decisions that don't align."[4] Though everyone can contribute to shaping the culture, Iverson believes that leadership is often responsible for destroying the culture and ethos of an organization. What leaders say must be supported through their actions. Building a healthy ethos in an organization is about its leaders embodying high character and integrity.

Dr. Marina Theodotou stresses that in order to build a healthy ethos and culture, a leader must be able to persuade the people. Effective communication is paramount for Dr. Theodotou when it comes to inspiring a team and building a healthy culture in an organization. She believes that if a leader cannot emotionally connect with the people who they are leading, then it will be a difficult challenge for that leader to establish a healthy culture. An emotional connection does not happen unless the leader can let actions speak louder than words. This is critical for building a healthy ethos. "Ethos is your reputation and your character, which gives credibility to your point. As Warren Buffet said, it takes years to build and a few seconds to demolish. How can you demonstrate your ethos? Do you deliver what you promised? Do your actions provide evidence of what you are promising others to deliver? Cultivate your ethos, guard it, and deploy it to make your point heard and embraced by others."[5]

Vulnerability plays a crucial role in accelerating how leaders connect with the people they are guiding. By openly sharing their own struggles, uncertainties, and authentic selves, leaders foster a sense of trust and relatability. This, in turn, creates a stronger bond with their staff and encourages a deeper commitment to the leader's vision and goals.

Building a healthy and effective ethos is undoubtedly one of the more difficult challenges any leader faces. It involves not only setting a clear and inspiring direction but also cultivating an environment where the staff feel valued and understood. Leading with vulnerability can significantly enhance this process. When senior leaders demonstrate openness and honesty, they are more likely to inspire confidence and loyalty, paving the way for greater collaboration and support.

Furthermore, this approach does more than just build trust; it accelerates progress toward achieving objectives. The genuine connections established through vulnerability can lead to quicker problem-solving, more innovative ideas, and a more cohesive team dynamic. Thus, while the journey of leadership is complex and demanding, embracing vulnerability can greatly improve both the effectiveness and efficiency with which leaders reach their goals.

Another significant benefit is the creation of an environment where mistakes and failures are discussed openly and constructively, rather than being viewed as deeply negative. In such an ethos, staff performance issues are addressed in a supportive and encouraging manner. The strong human connections that senior leaders foster with their teams lead to more transparent and meaningful conversations. This open dialogue not only enhances self-awareness among staff but also contributes to improved overall performance.

Monica Parker, in her provocative article "Embracing Vulnerability at Work Is Key to Employee Engagement", draws an intimate connection with a company's lack of vulnerability to its employees burning out. A working environment in which people don't feel free to be open or make mistakes is corrosive. She argues that people in these environments will do anything to avoid blame, and genuine accountability goes out of the window to be replaced by bullying and even trying to hurt the success of other employees. Trust and teamwork are eroded, and the workplace becomes somewhere to dread.

> A workforce that operates in this way is suffering from what psychologists call burnout: a state of blame, lethargy and negativity. This in turn can lead to individuals simply withdrawing from workplace life, or pushing themselves too much, neglecting their own needs as well as those of others. This is more common than you might think, in the US, for example, one study found that 70% of workers are disengaged from their work and "sleepwalking through their day." Worse still, 18% of those say they actively seek to undermine their co-workers' success.[6]

For Parker, the opposite of burnout is engagement. Engagement doesn't happen unless the ethos of the workplace is vulnerable. She says, "an engaged workforce can't be fashioned from the odd brainstorm or a staff ideas box. Stirring up real creativity takes a complete change of mindset. Companies need to embrace vulnerability and work with staff to be open with each other about ideas and emotions."[7]

Lisa Schmidt argues that a vulnerable ethos in a workplace is key for employees to thrive in a company. The reason for this is due to the fact that being vulnerable is the root of authentic and meaningful connection. It is the ability to reveal, in words and behavior, who we really are and what we genuinely think and feel. Schmidt believes that a vulnerable ethos benefits the company because its employees can bring their "full selves to work, with key outcomes including better quality output and more fulfilled workers. In fact, being able to reveal the breadth of our human experience (whether struggling as a single parent, having a mental health issue or experiencing overwhelm in a new role, for example) has been tied to enhanced feelings of self-worth, increased creativity and innovation, and deeper relationships, all of which benefit us both professionally and personally."[8]

To be honest, I find it easier to open up about my struggles, failures, and hardships during my sermons than I do when interacting with the staff. Speaking about these personal challenges in a sermon feels less intimate because it's delivered to a large audience in a public setting. This format allows me to share my experiences in a more controlled, one-way communication style, which, paradoxically, makes it easier for me to be open.

In contrast, sharing these same experiences with our staff feels more personal and requires a different level of vulnerability. When addressing a group of several hundred people, it's easier to maintain a certain emotional distance. However, with our staff, the interaction is much more intimate and direct, which makes it more challenging for me to be as open. This closer, more personal dynamic brings its own set of difficulties.

Despite these challenges, I understand that if we want to cultivate an environment where our staff feels comfortable embracing and discussing their own weaknesses, I need to lead by example. Being vulnerable about my own struggles is crucial in setting the tone for our team. It's important for me to step out of my comfort zone and share openly with our staff, demonstrating that vulnerability is not only acceptable but also valuable for growth and connection.

Years ago, I made the mistake of hiring an Executive Pastor (EP) without seeking input from our staff. The decision was made solely by the elder board and myself, without consulting the staff. In a turn of unfortunate events, we had to part ways with the Executive Pastor. It became clear that the staff had not been pleased with the hiring decision from the start.

To address this, I organized a voluntary staff meeting to openly discuss the situation. My goal was twofold: to allow the staff to voice their concerns about the EP hire and to present my side of the story, defending the decision that the elder board and I had made. I prepared thoroughly, ready to explain our choice based on the candidate's qualifications and experiences.

To my surprise, a large majority of the staff attended the meeting. I explained that the elder board and I believed the EP candidate was well qualified for the role and shared his resume and relevant experiences. However, the staff expressed their disappointment in not having had the opportunity to meet the candidate before the decision was finalized. They felt excluded from the process and hurt by the lack of consultation and communication.

Listening to their feedback, it became clear that the staff felt disrespected and undervalued because their input had not been considered in the hiring process. This realization was deeply unsettling. I took a moment to reflect on the situation, acknowledging their feelings and recognizing the impact of my oversight. To my surprise, the emotional weight of the situation overwhelmed me, and I found myself crying. It hit me just how much my actions had hurt the team and made them feel devalued. The realization of their disappointment and frustration was a heavy burden. I expressed my heartfelt regret, asked for their forgiveness, and promised to include them in the future hiring decision for our next EP.

True to my commitment, I ensured that the process of hiring our next EP involved the staff's input and approval. This collaborative approach led to the successful appointment of Steve, whose integration into our team has been remarkably smooth and positive.

Reflecting on this experience, I have come to understand that one of the most challenging aspects of leadership is addressing one's own mistakes, particularly when you are a senior leader. My initial reaction to such situations is often to try to cover up the error or justify the failure. However, I have learned from experience that this approach is not effective, especially in a church environment where transparency and trust are essential.

Admitting that I was wrong and seeking forgiveness from the staff was an incredibly vulnerable moment for me. It required a level of humility and openness that is difficult to embrace for some senior leaders. The staff was taken aback by my emotional response, but they were also grateful for my sincere apology. This moment of vulnerability helped rebuild trust and reassured them that they could continue to rely on me to lead with integrity. It was a poignant reminder of how essential it is for leaders to be honest and accountable, even when it feels uncomfortable. When church staff witnesses such vulnerability from their senior leaders, it empowers them to lead with the same openness and honesty in their own ministries. This, in turn, helps establish and maintain the vulnerable, weak ethos of the church.

When a senior leader sets an example by embracing vulnerability and openly acknowledging their own failures and weaknesses, it has a profound impact on the organizational culture. This level of transparency not only builds trust but also creates an environment where addressing staff issues—whether they pertain to performance, character, or integrity—is approached with greater openness and receptivity.

By showing that it's acceptable to admit mistakes and discuss personal shortcomings, the leader fosters a culture of mutual respect and honesty. Staff members are more likely to feel comfortable discussing their own challenges and seeking feedback when they see their leaders leading by example. This openness helps to break down barriers and reduce the fear of negative judgment, making it easier for staff to engage in meaningful conversations about improvement and growth.

Furthermore, when issues arise, staff are more inclined to listen to and collaborate with their managers, knowing that the feedback is coming from a place of genuine concern rather than criticism. This creates a more supportive and constructive atmosphere where problems can be addressed effectively, and solutions can be developed collaboratively. Ultimately, this approach strengthens the overall dynamic within the team, fostering a culture where continuous improvement and open communication are valued and practiced.

Ancy is a key member of our executive pastoral team, responsible for overseeing the church's student ministries, from birth through high school. She leads a team of six staff members at Metro Community Church. Ancy is a visionary leader with one of the most creative minds I've ever encountered. I deeply value her insights, and I always make sure she's part of our think tank sessions because her contributions are invaluable.

However, there were some challenges that affected Ancy's leadership, which her supervisor, Steve, our EP, needed to address. Steve informed her that they needed to have a difficult conversation. Both Steve and I had serious concerns about Ancy's ability to lead effectively in conflict situations. He asked me to join the meeting, not only to share my perspective but also to offer encouragement and support if he came across too harshly.

When we met with Ancy, Steve began by expressing how much he valued and appreciated her contributions. However, he then addressed the issues that had arisen with some of her staff members who did not respond well to her leadership. Steve often had to step in and handle these situations, frequently bearing the brunt of the conflict himself.

He said, "Ancy, with the staff members you have strong relationships with, you're a ceiling raiser—you help them excel and achieve even greater things. But with those you struggle to connect with, there's no floor on how badly things can go." Steve pointed out that Ancy struggled with conflict resolution, often prioritizing making others feel good over delivering the hard truth. As a result, Steve had to play the "bad guy," stepping in to manage conflicts when Ancy couldn't.

He made it clear that he couldn't fully trust her in these challenging situations and emphasized that she needed to grow in her leadership to handle such conflicts more effectively. Steve provided several examples where he had to intervene on her behalf.

The tension in the room grew as I noticed Ancy becoming defensive, but she quickly composed herself and admitted, "You're right, I'm not good with confrontation. I'm not sure why, but I get easily intimidated when someone challenges or disagrees with me." I reassured her that it's natural to feel intimidated when a staff member disagrees or challenges our leadership. However, as leaders, we must be willing to stand our ground, especially when it comes to issues of character.

Steve shared that during his devotions, God had impressed upon him the importance of pursuing the fruit of the Spirit. While reflecting on this, God revealed to him that Ancy was struggling with bitterness, which was hindering her from fully embracing the fruits of the Spirit. When Steve asked Ancy if she was dealing with bitterness, she initially said she didn't think so. However, as we continued to discuss it, she soon realized that she was indeed struggling with bitterness, which was affecting her ability to lead effectively. This realization was a breakthrough for Ancy, and she broke down in tears as it all became clear to her.

After that meeting, Ancy spent considerable time reflecting on her calling and her role as a leader. She acknowledged that she had often struggled with self-doubt, particularly in her capacity as a preacher. For years, she had tried to find confidence within herself, constantly questioning whether she was good enough or capable enough to fulfill the responsibilities of her position. This internal struggle had frequently undermined her sense of purpose and effectiveness in ministry.

However, as she contemplated the feedback she received and sought clarity, Ancy came to a pivotal realization: her confidence should not rest in her own abilities or in the approval of others. Instead, it should be grounded in the fact that God had called her to be a pastor and preacher. This shift in perspective was transformative for Ancy. She recognized that her true strength and authority came from her divine calling, not from her own efforts or perceived shortcomings.

Embracing this truth, Ancy resolved to move forward with a renewed sense of purpose and assurance. She understood that while challenges and doubts would still arise, her confidence would now be rooted in the certainty that she was fulfilling God's will for her life. This newfound perspective empowered her to lead with greater conviction and to trust more fully in the guidance and support that comes from her faith.

This was undoubtedly a turning point for Ancy. After our meeting with Steve, she emerged as a different leader. Now, she preaches with an authority and boldness that I hadn't seen in her before. Ancy is far more confident and no longer shies away from confronting staff or others who challenge her. She embraces these situations, but more importantly, she's now focused on sharing the truth, even if it means others might not walk away feeling good. Her priority has shifted from seeking approval to upholding integrity and truth in her leadership.

I have always believed that Ancy was destined to become a senior pastor. Her visionary leadership qualities make her an ideal candidate for such a role. Despite this, whenever I shared my belief with Ancy, she would often voice doubts and uncertainties about her future as a senior pastor. She struggled to envision herself in that position, even though her talents and potential were evident.

After our meeting with Steve, she has fully embraced the possibility of becoming a senior pastor and is actively pursuing such a role within our denomination. This shift in her perspective is remarkable. Steve, our EP, has been instrumental in this transformation. He demonstrated deep affection for Ancy by being exceptionally honest and vulnerable with her, a testament to the honest, supportive culture we strive to maintain within our church.

Our church's ethos of vulnerability and weakness provided Ancy with a unique opportunity for growth. Through Steve's candid feedback and our supportive environment, Ancy developed a greater sense of self-awareness. This process has not only helped her excel in her current role at Metro but also bolstered her confidence in her calling to become a senior pastor.

Reflecting on this, I often wonder about the impact of our church's approach. If we hadn't fostered an environment where weakness is embraced, would Ancy have been able to grow from such a challenging confrontation with her boss? In a more traditional or less supportive church setting, a meeting like the one we had could have been devastating, potentially leading her to question her calling and possibly even abandon her ministry altogether due to discouragement.

Our church's commitment to a culture of vulnerability has clearly enabled Ancy to thrive, not just in her current position but also in her pursuit of the broader vision God has for her life. It's a powerful reminder of how a supportive and vulnerable environment can make a profound difference in the development of leaders.

There is a significant crisis among pastors today, with many leaving the ministry due to burnout or discouragement. According to Barna Research from March 2022, 42 percent of pastors have considered quitting full-time ministry, primarily due to stress and loneliness.[9] The reasons behind these feelings are varied, but imagine a scenario where pastors could work within a church staff where they felt comfortable openly sharing their stresses and loneliness, and where they experienced genuine support and solidarity from their colleagues.

After her meeting with Steve and me, Ancy could have easily felt overwhelmed and isolated. She might have felt lonely, believing that no one understood her struggles, or stressed about the need to improve her performance. These reactions are common among pastors facing performance evaluations. However, for Ancy, this moment became a defining one. She grew in self-awareness, openly confronting her pain and struggles with Steve, myself, and most importantly, with God. As a result, she now leads with a renewed sense of authority, confident in the calling she believes God has given her. Witnessing this transformation is truly inspiring.

Creating a vulnerable ethos where staff openly model and embrace their weaknesses sets a transformative example for the entire congregation. When church leaders are willing to show their weaknesses and openly discuss their struggles, it cultivates an environment of authenticity and support. This openness encourages the entire congregation to follow suit, embracing their own imperfections and challenges.

In such a setting, people are not only more willing to be honest about their struggles but also more likely to experience the perfect strength of God that comes from embracing our weaknesses. This spiritual strength enables individuals to face life's challenges with a sense of resilience and empowerment that feels almost superhuman.

I see this remarkable transformation in Ancy and many others in our church. They have embraced this approach and, as a result, have experienced a deepened sense of authority and purpose. This shift not only enhances their personal growth but also strengthens the entire community, creating a vibrant, vulnerable environment where everyone can thrive in their journey of faith.

The Nuts and Bolts of Building and Sustaining
a Vulnerable Church Staff Ethos

The journey toward fostering vulnerability within a church staff is not a linear or predictable process. Much of the responsibility for creating this environment falls on the senior and executive pastors. When these leaders model vulnerability and openness, it sets a powerful example that encourages the entire staff to adopt a similar ethos organically.

To support this development, I implement several key practices with our church staff. We gather weekly for staff meetings where we focus on building community and fostering open communication. These meetings provide a regular opportunity for staff members to share their experiences, challenges, and successes in a supportive environment.

In addition to our weekly meetings, we also hold an annual retreat where the entire staff can step away from the daily routine and engage in deeper, more meaningful interactions. This retreat is designed to strengthen our relationships, deepen our sense of community, and provide space for reflection and being vulnerable with one another.

Regular activities and initiatives are also part of our approach to cultivating vulnerability. These activities are aimed at building trust and encouraging staff members to be open about their struggles and aspirations. By consistently practicing these activities, we create an environment where vulnerability is not just encouraged but embraced as a fundamental aspect of our staff and church culture.

1. Quarterly Check In

    We dedicate an entire staff meeting exclusively to discussing how we're doing. This is our only agenda item, and it often takes the full duration of the meeting, sometimes even running over, due to the depth of openness and vulnerability with which our team shares their struggles. Vulnerability is a fundamental aspect of our staff ethos, so it's natural for everyone to be candid with one another. In the early years of our church, I would often start the conversation to set a tone of openness. However, as vulnerability has become deeply embedded in our staff culture, it really doesn't matter who starts. What's essential is that we have this dedicated time for honest sharing. We typically frame our conversation around the question, "How goes it with your soul?"

    This quarterly check-in often provides both the executive pastor and me with valuable insights into how we can better support our staff, particularly those who might be experiencing challenging times. By openly discussing how everyone is doing, we gain a clearer understanding of individual struggles and needs. This not only helps us identify areas where additional support or resources might be required but also enables us to tailor our approach to addressing specific issues. It's an opportunity for us to be more responsive and proactive in creating an environment that supports everyone's well-being, ensuring that we are effectively meeting the needs of our team members during their most difficult moments.

2. Biweekly Sharing and Discussion of Prayer Requests

Prayer is a vital component of our weekly staff meetings. We start each meeting with a moment of silence to help us center ourselves. Recognizing the value of mutual support through prayer, we also allocate time biweekly at the end of our meetings for staff members to form small groups of three or four. In these groups, we share prayer requests, discuss our personal challenges, and ask for support. This practice naturally fosters a sense of community and encouragement, as team members come together to uplift one another. It's a meaningful way to deepen our connections and offer staff members to be vulnerable with one another.

We also maintain a dedicated chat room called "Staff Prayer Requests." This space is specifically designed for staff members to share their prayer needs and personal updates in real time. Whenever someone has a request or an update they want to share, they post it in this chat room. This practice ensures that everyone stays informed about what's going on in each other's lives and can offer support and encouragement accordingly. By keeping the lines of communication open, we foster a stronger sense of community and ensure that we're all aware of the various challenges and joys our colleagues are experiencing.

3. Speaking Truth in Love

I encourage our staff to actively seek out opportunities to address potential blind spots in each other's leadership. Since we work closely together for extended periods, we often become aware of areas for improvement that others may not recognize. While this kind of feedback can be uncomfortable, it's a valuable part of our growth process. Although some staff members naturally take the initiative to receive this feedback, most do not. To ensure that everyone benefits from this practice, I make it a point to pair staff members up annually, typically during our retreat. Before the retreat, I assign each person a partner and inform them of who they will be providing feedback to. This gives them time to prepare, pray, and seek guidance. This process helps foster a culture of honesty and support, ultimately strengthening our team.

Initially, this practice was met with some resistance. One staff member expressed a need for more guidance, suggesting that we should require everyone to offer encouragement before sharing any critical feedback. I reassured them that our church's culture of vulnerability would address this concern naturally.

After the session, the same staff member approached me again, this time to suggest that we do this more often. The entire staff found it to be incredibly valuable. Sharing truth in love has become a cherished time for our staff to grow in greater self-awareness. While the feedback shared is sometimes not new, it often helps staff members explore these truths more deeply, offering valuable insights and growth.

A few years ago, I paired Steve, our EP, with David, our most respected pastor on staff. During their discussion, David challenged Steve by suggesting that if he were Jesus, he wouldn't have chosen the same twelve disciples that Jesus did. David's point was to encourage Steve to look beyond just hiring people with exceptional talent and to be more mindful of those on the fringe, similar to how Jesus chose individuals who were marginalized rather than superstars.

This conversation proved to be incredibly valuable for Steve. It served as a powerful reminder of the importance of seeking spiritual wisdom and discernment from God when making decisions about who to hire.

I paired up with Timm, Metro's Communication Director. During our conversation, Timm shared that I should never compare myself to friends who have achieved more on paper. Having been fortunate to be close friends with and mentored by some remarkable individuals, Timm was concerned that I might find myself measuring my achievements against theirs. Timm said, "Peter, don't compare yourself to them; stay focused on pastoring and leading Metro Community Church."

I deeply appreciated Timm's reminder. Although I've made great strides in avoiding comparisons with my illustrious friends, his words reinforced how much my staff values and supports me. It was a poignant reminder of the importance of staying true to the path God has set for me and finding contentment with it.

Pairing staff members to offer honest, constructive feedback with each other has proven to be profoundly rewarding for our team's growth in self-awareness. This practice allows us to delve deeply into personal and professional development, fostering a richer understanding of ourselves and each other. It's a testament to our church's commitment to embracing vulnerability and recognizing the value in acknowledging and addressing weaknesses.

Such an approach is only feasible in a church that genuinely values and supports the embracing of weakness. A church that does not have this ethos would likely struggle with maintaining such an open and honest practice. Our commitment to this process highlights how important it is for us to create an environment where personal growth and self-awareness are encouraged and supported, regardless of the discomfort that might come with it.

4. Affirmation Time

Hebrews 10:24 tells us, "Let us consider how we may spur one another on toward love and good deeds, not giving up meeting together, as some are in the habit of doing, but encouraging one another—and all the more as you see the Day approaching."

At our annual staff retreat, we make it a point to go around and affirm one another. This process, which involves the entire staff, can take hours, but it's crucial for building each other up. In a culture where negativity often overshadows positivity, especially in ministry, we rarely receive affirmation. This annual practice serves as a powerful reminder of the importance of being encouraged. It fosters greater unity among the staff, as they share vulnerably about the qualities they admire in each member and the positive impact they've made.

5. Speak Prophetically

As a spiritual community, our church staff is called to speak prophetically into each other's lives, nurturing and encouraging one another in our shared mission. A few times a year, we set aside dedicated moments for this purpose. During these sessions, we break into small groups of three or four, creating an intimate and supportive environment.

In these groups, we take time to pray and seek the guidance of the Holy Spirit, inviting Him to speak through us. We share prophetic words and offer encouragement, focusing on uplifting each other and addressing the unique needs and strengths of each staff member. These moments are profoundly beneficial, as they not only help us grow in our spiritual gifts but also deepen our connections and foster a greater sense of unity within the team.

Additionally, these prophetic prayers minister deeply to those who receive them, addressing areas where they may be struggling. Hearing from God directly through the prophetic prayer of the staff provides a concrete experience of God speaking to us, offering clarity and reassurance in our personal and professional lives.

6. Foot Washing

In John 13:1–17, Jesus demonstrates a powerful lesson in humility and service by washing His disciples' feet. He encourages us to follow His example, emphasizing the importance of serving one another.

In the first century, washing feet was a task typically reserved for slaves. People walked in sandals and often encountered filth, including dirt and waste, on their journeys. Therefore, foot washing was considered a menial and undesirable job, performed by those in the lowest positions. When Jesus chose to wash His disciples' feet, He was embodying the role of a slave, performing an act that highlighted His commitment to serving them.

Peter's reaction to Jesus washing his feet—"No, you shall never wash my feet"—reflects the shock and indignation such an act provoked. Jesus' response, "Unless I wash you, you have no part with me," underscores the significance of this humble act and Jesus' commitment to Peter and the other disciples.[10]

By washing His disciples' feet, Jesus was illustrating the counter intuitive nature of the Kingdom of God compared to worldly values. This act of service was a profound expression of His love and commitment. Even as He prepared to return to the Father in heaven, Jesus wanted His disciples to understand the depth of His love and the essence of true leadership and service.

When our staff washes each other's feet, it symbolizes our deep commitment to love and serve one another. We often express what a privilege it is to participate in this act, pledging to support each other in all circumstances. The ceremony frequently leaves us with tearful eyes, moved by the profound humility of the gesture.

Our annual staff retreat culminates with a meaningful foot-washing ceremony, a tradition that reflects Jesus' profound act of service to His disciples. This final activity not only reminds us of His humility and dedication but also inspires our team to carry this spirit of service into our relationships with one another and within the ministry teams we lead.

Concluding Remarks

The church staff serve as the frontline soldiers in carrying out the mission of embracing vulnerability within the church. This role is particularly challenging because church culture often reflects the prevailing values of strength, success, and self-sufficiency that dominate the world today. To truly fulfill their mission, staff must lead by example, creating and nurturing safe spaces where vulnerability is not only accepted but encouraged.

If the staff fails to model this openness and authenticity, the congregation will struggle to develop into a weak church. For the church to become a place where individuals feel free to express their weaknesses and seek support, it is essential that the staff first embody these principles themselves. Their willingness to acknowledge and embrace their own weaknesses sets a powerful precedent for the entire community.

Thus, the ethos of the church staff must center around embracing their own imperfections and weaknesses. This commitment is not just about personal growth but about fostering a church environment where every member feels empowered to engage with their own weaknesses. When staff members model this kind of authentic engagement, they inspire the congregation to do the same, leading to a more compassionate and unified church. Ultimately, by embracing their own weaknesses, church staff can profoundly impact the broader church community, helping to cultivate a culture where vulnerability is seen as a strength and a path to deeper connection and spiritual growth.

Notes

1. Jane Sparrow, "Company Ethos Should Be a Key Priority for Leaders Right Now," *Forbes.com*, September 28, 2022, accessed January 21, 2023, https://www.forbes.com/sites/janesparrow/2022/09/28/company-ethos-should-be-a-key-priority-for-leaders-right-now/?sh=cd677d876165.

2. (Matthew 26:36–38 NIV).

3. Erick, Iverson, "The Importance of Honing Your Company's Cultural Ethos," *Fastcompany.com*, May 5, 2022, accessed January 21, 2023, https://www.fastcompany .com/90747729/the-importance-of-honing-your-companys-cultural-ethos.

4. Ibid.

5. Marina Theodotou, "Leadership Blueprint: Persuade Like Aristotle," *eLearning Industry*, October 20, 2022, accessed March 4, 2023, https://elearningindustry.com/ leadership-blueprint-persuade-like-aristotle-cultivate-ethos-pathos-logos.

6. Monica Parker, "Embracing Vulnerability at Work is Key to Employee Engagement," *The Guardian*, September 30, 2013, accessed March 4, 2023, https://www .theguardian.com/sustainable-business/embrace-vulnerabilty-workplace-employee -engagement.

7. Ibid.

8. Lisa Schmidt, "Vulnerability in the Workplace: A Leadership Skill," *World of Work Project*, January 2020, accessed March 4, 2023, https://worldofwork.io/2020/01 /vulnerability-in-the-workplace/#:~:text=Being%20genuinely%20vulnerable%20in %20the,welcomes%20and%20recognizes%20genuine%20openness.

9. Barna Group, "Pastors Share Top Reasons They've Considered Quitting Ministry in the Past Year," *Barna*, April 27, 2022, accessed August 18, 2024, https://www .barna.com/research/pastors-quitting-ministry/.

10. John 13:8.

Conclusion

We have embarked on a transformative journey, not merely dreaming about what a Weak Church could look like, but providing you with practical, tangible examples to guide you in building a church that truly harnesses God's strength made perfect in our weakness. The question is: Is this an easy task? Absolutely not! It's a heavy lift, and one that demands not only hard work, but perseverance, faith, and a willingness to endure discomfort.

Anything of lasting value requires significant effort, and leading a Weak Church is no different. It's a calling that will challenge you, stretch your limits, and at times, test your resolve. But here's the beautiful truth—leading a church where God's power shines through human weakness is worth every sacrifice. To embrace this model of leadership is not for the faint-hearted or those seeking a path of least resistance. It calls for extraordinary courage— the courage to be vulnerable in front of those you are leading, to admit when you don't have all the answers, and to trust God's sufficiency where your own strength falls short.

In a world that often glorifies power, dominance, and self-sufficiency, it takes radical faith to guide a church toward a different paradigm—one where dependence on God is the foundation. It's a leadership that isn't about wielding control or projecting invincibility, but about creating a space where God's grace and power can flow through the brokenness, flaws, and limitations of both the leaders and the congregation.

So, is it a high calling? Absolutely. But it's one that carries profound rewards—both in the lives of the people you lead and in your own spiritual journey as you witness God do what only He can do. To lead a Weak Church is to lean into the paradox that in our weakness, He is strong, and that in relinquishing our obsession with strength, we find true freedom.

This is not a matter to be taken lightly, nor is it something to simply ponder over for an extended period of time. The reality is already upon us—studies clearly show that people are leaving the church, or at the very least, positioning themselves to do so. The younger generation, particularly Gen Z, is finding little reason to see the church as a place worthy of their commitment or time. This isn't just a minor issue; it's a silent but growing crisis within the church today. And it demands a response marked by urgency from pastors and church leaders alike.

We cannot afford to sit idly by or rely on outdated models of ministry that no longer resonate with the world around us. While I am not claiming that *The Weak Church* is the sole solution or the definitive model for every church, I do firmly believe that if we want to minister effectively, using God's perfect strength, then embracing the principles of a Weak Church is one crucial way forward.

In earlier chapters, I shared that one of the motivations behind planting Metro Community Church was to create a welcoming home for individuals like my sister Susan, who has a learning disability. Growing up, Susan never felt fully embraced or loved by the churches we attended, and I regretfully admit that I was among those who hesitated to bring her church due to her perceived weaknesses. This ultimately led her to walk away from the church altogether.

I never imagined that she would find her way back. Yet, as I write this concluding chapter, my heart is filled with gratitude and awe. For several months now, Susan, along with her husband and my nephew, who has autism, has been faithfully attending Metro Community Church. I have been given another chance! My sister Susan is now a part of the congregation I pastor, and that is a blessing beyond words.

Our church community has welcomed them with open arms, showering them with the love and acceptance they had long been denied. Every Sunday, they make the long commute from Bedford-Stuyvesant, Brooklyn to join us, willing to travel the distance to be part of a Weak Church. This is nothing short of a miracle, a testament to God's grace, and a powerful reminder of the urgent need for more Weak Churches around the world. The fact that Susan, after so many years, has found a spiritual home is both a personal joy and a poignant illustration of how churches that embrace vulnerability, authenticity, and God's strength in weakness can bring healing and restoration to those who've felt forgotten.

This isn't just a call to reimagine church for the sake of change. It's not about adopting trendy models or seeking to be more culturally relevant at the expense of spiritual depth. It's about recognizing that our strength, as individuals and as church communities, is not in how polished our programs are, or how seamlessly we can run Sunday services, or even how well we can articulate theological points. Our strength comes when we surrender our need to control and project an image of perfection. It comes when we allow ourselves to be vulnerable—first before God, and then before the people we are called to serve. This is what it means to be a Weak Church.

The current crisis of disengagement, especially among younger generations, cannot be solved by simply modernizing our worship or upgrading our technology. Many pastors and church leaders have tried this approach, and while it may have temporarily filled pews, it hasn't filled hearts. People are searching for something deeper. They want to know that the church is a place where they can bring their whole selves—their doubts, their fears, their imperfections—and still be accepted and loved. They want to know that it's okay to be weak, because that's when God's strength can truly shine.

And yet, this is where many churches are missing the mark. Too often, churches project an image of self-sufficiency, of having all the answers, of leaders who seem untouchable, above the struggles that their congregants face. But what if, instead of presenting a facade of strength, we led with our weakness? What if pastors and leaders were willing to be vulnerable, to share their own struggles and limitations, even from the pulpit? What if we created a culture where the message wasn't "come to church to be perfect" but "come to church to encounter a perfect God who meets us in our imperfection"?

Leading a Weak Church isn't about giving up or lowering the bar of what we expect from our people. It's about raising the bar on our dependence on God. It's about embracing the paradox that it's only when we stop trying to do everything in our own strength that we can experience the fullness of His. This requires a radical shift in how we think about leadership and ministry. It's not about being the most dynamic, the most charismatic, or the most well-resourced leader. It's about being the most surrendered.

This path is not an easy one. It requires immense courage to lead from a place of weakness. It requires vulnerability to stand before your congregation and admit that you don't have all the answers, that you struggle, that you need God just as much as they do. But it is in this very act of vulnerability that the church can become a place where God's grace and strength are truly magnified.

Pastors and leaders, I urge you to consider this seriously. The time for waiting is over. The Church must act with a renewed sense of urgency to meet the growing needs and spiritual hunger of those both within and beyond its walls. This isn't just about survival—it's about thriving in a way that aligns with God's design for His church. Becoming a Weak Church doesn't mean becoming ineffective or powerless; it means tapping into a power far greater than anything we could ever muster on our own.

The future of the church hinges on our response to this pivotal moment. Will we persist with the status quo, relying on minor adjustments to attract people to our congregation? Or will we summon the courage to lead in a new direction, embracing humility and acknowledging our weaknesses, so that God's strength can be made perfect within us? The choice is ours, but the time for choosing is now!

The call to embrace the Weak Church is not merely a strategy—it's a profound shift in how we lead. It invites us to move with vulnerability, humility, and complete reliance on God's power instead of our own. This is a call to reimagine the church as a community where weakness becomes a gateway to strength, surrender leads to transformation, and God's grace flows most powerfully through our brokenness. The journey ahead may be difficult, but it offers the possibility of deep spiritual renewal, authentic connection, and lasting impact. Now is the time to step forward, to embrace this redefinition of leadership and church life. In doing so, we will discover that it is in our willingness to be weak that God's strength can truly shine, renewing both the church and those we are called to serve. Let us as pastors and church leaders move forward with courage, faith, and a deep trust that in our weakness, He is truly strong!

Bibliography

Anderson, Ray S. *The Soul of Ministry*. Louisville: Westminster John Knox Press, 1997.

Baldo Jose L. *Mother Teresa In My Own Words*. New York: Random House Value Publishing, 1989.

Barna Group. *Gen Z Volume 2*. A Barna Report and Impact 360 Institute, 2021.

Barna Group. "Pastors Share Top Reasons They've Considered Quitting Ministry in the Past Year." *Barna*. April 27, 2022. Accessed August 18, 2024. https://www.barna.com/research/pastors-quitting-ministry/.

Barna Group. "Pastors, Too, Grapple with Thoughts of Suicide, Self Harm." *Barna*. September 12, 2024. Accessed December 2, 2024. https://www.barna.com/research/pastors-thoughts-suicide-self-harm/.

Besley, Sharon. "Why You Click With Certain People." *Mind and Body*. August 16, 2018. Accessed May 1, 2021. https://greatergood.berkeley.edu/article/item/why_you_click_with_certain_people.

Brown, Brene. *I Thought It Was Just Me*. New York: Penguin Random House, 2007.

Brown, Brene. *The Gifts of Imperfection*. Minnesota: Hazelden Publishing, 2010.

Butcher, Kevin. *Free*. Grand Rapids: NAV Press, 2021.

Chodron, Pema. *The Places That Scare You*. Boston: Shambhala Publication, 2001.

Collins, Jim. *Good to Great*. New York: Harper Collins Publishing, 2001.

Coyle, Daniel. "How Showing Vulnerability Helps Build Stronger Teams." *Ideas.Ted.com*. February 20, 2018. Accessed January 21, 2023. https://ideas.ted.com/how-showing-vulnerability-helps-build-a-stronger-team/.

Dale, Bruner Fredrick. *Matthew: A Commentary, Volume 2. The Churchbook, Matthew 13-28*. Grand Rapids: Eerdmans Publishing, 1987.

Decker, Bert. *You've Got to Be Believed to be Heard*. New York: St. Martin's Press, 2008.

Emiliani, Robin. "Keeping it Real: Gen Z's Hunger for Authentic Marketing and Purpose Driven Brands." *Catalyst*. January 22, 2023. Accessed September 9, 2024. https://catalystmarketing.io/blog/gen-zs-hunger-for-authentic-marketing-and-purpose-driven-brands/.

Geyen, Monica. "Is The Church Breeding Loneliness?" *Desiring God*. April 17, 2019. Accessed January 21, 2023. https://www.desiringgod.org/articles/is-the-church-breeding-loneliness.

Goleman, Daniel. *Social Intelligence: The New Science of Human Relationships*. New York: Random House/Bantam Dell, 2006.

Heller, Dov. "Eight Habits of Emotionally Healthy People." *AISH*. Accessed January 21, 2023. https://aish.com/eight-habits-of-emotionally-healthy-people/.

Hill, Daniel. *White Awake*. Downers Grove: Intervarsity Press, 2017.

Hill, Daniel. *White Lies*. Grand Rapids: Zondervan Books, 2020.

Hoglen, Jeff. "Overcoming Fear of Failure: Plant a Thriving Church." *Churchplanting.com*. May 8, 2023. Accessed September 9, 2024. https://churchplanting.com/overcome-the-fear-of-failure-in-church-planting/#:~:text=Estimates%20vary%20between%2050%25%2D,first%20few%20months%20of%20operation.

Huguley, Ryan. "3 Reasons Pastors Need to Be Vulnerable." *Christianity.com*. August 3, 2014. Accessed December 13, 2021. https://www.christianity.com/church/pastors/3-reasons-pastors-need-to-be-vulnerable-and-3-cautions.html.

Iverson, Erick. "The Importance of Honing Your Company's Cultural Ethos." *Fastcompany.com*. May 5, 2022. Accessed January 21, 2023. https://www.fastcompany.com/90747729/the-importance-of-honing-your-companys-cultural-ethos.

Karen, Robert. "Shame." *The Atlantic Monthly*, February 2009. Accessed May 4, 2021. http://www.empoweringpeople.net/shame/shame.pdf.

Kochhar, Rakesh and Moslimani, Mohamad. "Wealth Gaps Across Racial and Ethnic Groups." *Pew Research*. December 2, 2023. Accessed July 24, 2024. https://www.pewresearch.org/2023/12/04/wealth-gaps-across-racial-and-ethnic-groups/#:~:text=Asian%20households%20overall%20had%20more,(%2427%2C100)%20was%20much%20less.\.

Lawson, Steven J. "Why Is Preaching Important For Healthy Churches." *Table Talk*. October 4, 2021. Accessed November 5, 2021. https://tabletalkmagazine.com/posts/why-is-the-preaching-of-gods-word-vital-for-the-health-of-the-local-church/.

Lifeway Research. "Most Teenagers Drop Out Of Church When They Become Young Adults." *Lifeway Research*. January 15, 2019. Accessed May 1, 2021. https://lifewayresearch.com/2019/01/15/most-teenagers-drop-out-of-church-as-young-adults/.

Linnaberry, Eileen. "Why Your Leadership Development Program Isn't Working, And What To Do About It." *Vantage Leadership*. 2021. Accessed January 21, 2023. https://www.vantageleadership.com/our-blog/leadership-development-programs-not-delivering-results/.

McNeil, Brenda Salter. *Roadmap to Reconciliation 2.0.* Downers Grove: InterVarsity Press, 2020.

McWilliams James. "Bryan Stevenson on What Well-Meaning White People Need to Know About Race." *Pacific Standard.* February 19, 2019. Accessed January 21, 2023. https://psmag.com/magazine/bryan-stevenson-ps-interview.

Mitchell, Michal. "Eight Habits that Destroy Your Emotional Well Being." *Psy2Go.* September 4, 2020. Accessed January 21, 2023. https://psych2go.net/8-habits-that-destroy-your-emotional-well-being/.

Moss, Carter. "5 Mistakes the Ruin Small Groups." *Smallgroups.com.* February 23, 2015. Accessed November 5, 2021. https://www.smallgroups.com/articles/2015/5-mistakes-that-ruin-small-groups.html.

Nguyen, Viet Thanh. "Asian Americans Are Still Caught in the Trap of the 'Model Minority' Stereotype. And It Creates Inequality for All." *Time.* June 26, 2020. Accessed July 24, 2024, https://time.com/5859206/anti-asian-racism-america/.

Nouwen, Henri. *In the Name of Jesus: Reflections on Christian Leadership.* New York: Crossroad Publishing, 1989.

Parker, Monica. "Embracing Vulnerability at Work is Key to Employee Engagement." *The Guardian.* September 30, 2013. Accessed March 4, 2023. https://www.theguardian.com/sustainable-business/embrace-vulnerabilty-workplace-employee-engagement.

Reimer, Rob. *Soul Care.* Franklin: Carpenter's Son Publishing, 2016.

Sandstrom, Aleksandra . "In US, Decline of Christianity Continues at a Rapid Pace." *Pew Research Center*, October 17, 2019. Accessed May 1, 2021. https://www.pewforum.org/2019/10/17/in-u-s-decline-of-christianity-continues-at-rapid-pace/.

Scazzero, Peter. *Emotionally Healthy Spirituality.* Grand Rapids: Zondervan, 2006.

Scazzero, Peter. *Emotionally Healthy Leader.* Grand Rapids: Zondervan, 2015.

Scazzero, Peter. *Emotionally Healthy Discipleship.* Grand Rapids: Zondervan Reflective, 2021.

Schmidt, Lisa. "Vulnerability in the Workplace: A Leadership Skill." *World of Work Project.* January 2020. Accessed March 4, 2023. https://worldofwork.io/2020/01/vulnerability-in-theworkplace/#:~:text=Being%20genuinely%20vulnerable%20in%20the,welcomes%20and%20recognizes%20genuine%20openness.

Sider, Ron. *Rich Christians in an Age of Hunger.* Dallas: Word Publishing, 1997.

Smith, Mandy. *The Vulnerable Pastor.* Downers Grove: Intervarsity Press, 2015.

Smith, Reid. "5 Ways to Cultivate Vulnerability in Your Small Group." *Lifeway Research.* September 24, 2019. Accessed May 4, 2021. https://lifewayresearch.com/2019/09/24/5-ways-to-cultivate-vulnerability-in-your-small-group/.

Sparrow, Jane. "Company Ethos Should Be a Key Priority for Leaders Right Now." *Forbes.* September 28, 2022. Accessed January 21, 2023. https://www.forbes.com/sites/janesparrow/2022/09/28/company-ethos-should-be-a-key-priority-for-leaders-right-now/?sh=cd677d876165.

"Springtide Research." *ROTW.com*. 2021. Accessed December 13, 2021. https://www.rotw.com/get-facts/85-young-people-ages-12-25-don%E2%80%99t-see-their-church-place-they-can-turn-times-trouble.

Stern, Richard. *The Hole in Our Gospel*. Nashville: Thomas Nelson Publishing, 2009.

Swanson David. *Rediscipling the White Church*. Downers Grove: Intervarsity Press, 2020.

Tenx10. "With 1 Million Leaving the Church Every Year, Is Gen Z the Faithless Generation?" *Sojourners*. February 26, 2024. Accessed December 2, 2024, https://sojo.net/articles/sponsored/1-million-leaving-church-every-year-gen-z-faithless-generation.

Teresa, Mother. *The Love of Christ*. San Francisco: Harper and Row, 1982.

Theodotou, Marina. "Leadership Blueprint: Persuade Like Aristotle." *eLearning Industry*. October 20, 2022. Accessed March 4, 2024. https://elearningindustry.com/leadership-blueprint-persuade-like-aristotle-cultivate-ethos-pathos-logos.

Thompson, Curt. *The Soul of Shame*. Downers Grove: IVP, 2015.

Thompson, Curt. "New Canaan Society National Conference." Omni Orlando Resort, Florida. March 1–3, 2019. Accessed December 13, 2021. https://www.youtube.com/watch?v=6J6i-pSQGqc.

Volstad, Amy. "Emotionally Healthy Vs. Spiritually Healthy." *Christian Counselors Collaborative*. June 27, 2017. Accessed January 21, 2023. https://www.cccpgh.org/emotionally-healthy-vs-spiritually-healthy/.

Wallis, Jim. "Who Is My Neighbor?" *Sojourners Magazine*. November 1994.

Warren, Rick. "Vulnerability: A Forgotten Virtue of Great Leadership." *Pastors.com*. April 11, 2016. Accessed March 4, 2023. https://pastors.com/vulnerability-forgotten-virtue-great-leadership/.

Wentz, Myles. "Jemar Tisby: Three Words Should Guide Our Pursuit of Racial Justice." *Christianity Today*. June 10, 2021. Accessed March 4, 2023. https://www.christianitytoday.com/ct/2021/june-web-only/jemar-tisby-how-fight-racism-three-words.html.

White, Stephen P. "Why We Need A Church That Is Poor And For The Poor." *Americamagazine.org*. September 08, 2015. Accessed January 21, 2023. https://www.americamagazine.org/issue/213/they-know-suffering-christ?gclid=CjwKCAiA_6yfBhBNEiwAkmXy56QqlBhG-Sp1MmkRkyAkxYOOln_O032M5ZuF-nMnd_6G98joBEcZq0xoCw_gQAvD_BwE/.

Wilson, Sandra D. *Released From Shame: Moving Beyond the Pain of the Past*. Downers Grove, IL: Intervarsity Press, 2002.

"10 Truths of Churches That Do A Great Job With Leadership Development." *Leadnet.org*. June 11, 2019. Accessed May 4, 2021. https://leadnet.org/10-truths-of-churches-that-do-a-great-job-with-leadership-development-part-2/.

"The Most Segregated Hour in America – Martin Luther King Jr." *YouTube*, uploaded by Jason Tripp. April 29, 2014. Accessed on July 14, 2024. https://www.youtube.com/watch?v=1q881g1L_d8.

Index

About the Author

Peter Ahn is the founder and lead pastor of Metro Community Church, a thriving, multi-ethnic congregation in Englewood, New Jersey. Since its inception, Metro's guiding philosophy has centered around the concept of embracing weakness. Over the past two decades, he has been able to test, learn, and hone the fundamental principles that define a "weak church." As a result, he has traveled around the world hosting Weak Church conferences and actively mentors staff and fellow pastors and church leaders in adopting this approach. Peter is also a co-host of a weekly podcast "Weak Pastor," where he explores the Christian faith through the lens of vulnerability. Peter is a graduate of Fuller Theological Seminary and Alliance Theological Seminary and holds a Doctroate of Ministry in Global Leadership. He resides in Northern New Jersey with his wife, Jenny, and their three incredible children—Christina, Kayla, and Christian.